T0356646

THE
SACRED HEART

A LOVE FOR ALL TIMES

THE SACRED HEART

A LOVE FOR ALL TIMES

DAWN EDEN GOLDSTEIN

LOYOLA PRESS.
A JESUIT MINISTRY

LOYOLA PRESS.
A JESUIT MINISTRY

www.loyolapress.com

Copyright © 2025 by Dawn Eden Goldstein
All rights reserved.

Scripture texts in this work are taken from the New American Bible, Revised Edition © 1970, 1986, 1991, 2010 by Confraternity of Christian Doctrine, Inc., Washington, DC, and are used by permission of the copyright owner. All rights reserved. No part of the New American Bible may be reproduced in any form without permission in writing from the copyright owner.

Cover art credit: The Crosiers/Gene Plaisted, OSC
p. viii image credit: Sedmak/iStock/Getty Images
Back cover author photo: James Martone

ISBN: 978-0-8294-5874-9
Library of Congress Control Number: 2024946345

Published in Chicago, IL
Printed in the United States of America
24 25 26 27 28 29 30 31 32 33 Versa 10 9 8 7 6 5 4 3 2 1

To William Doino Jr.,
my cherished friend in the Heart of Jesus,
with love, prayers, and gratitude always.

Contents

Sacred Heart of Jesus by Pompeo Batoni. Church of the Gesù, Rome.

Introduction

In December 2023, on my first visit to Rome since the COVID-19 pandemic, I paid my respects at Jesuit Father Pedro Arrupe's tomb in the Church of the Gesù, the mother church of the Society of Jesus. Then I made my way directly back to the Chapel of the Sacred Heart, just to the right of the church's main altar. A sign at its entrance carried an implicit warning for photographers and chattering tourists, stating in seven languages, "This place is exclusively for prayer."

As I entered the chapel, I was delighted to find no one else kneeling before the treasure hanging upon its back wall. *Good*, I thought. I would have a moment alone with the most celebrated painting of the Sacred Heart in all history.

The painting is by Pompeo Batoni, who was one of Rome's most sought-after portrait artists. In 1767, two years after Pope Clement XIII approved devotion to the Sacred Heart of Jesus, Batoni was commissioned by Father Domenico Maria Saverio Calvi, SJ, to paint the Sacred Heart. Perhaps it is because of the artist's expertise in portraiture that the image, although certainly devotional, strikes the viewer more as a depiction of a family member than as an icon. It is, in a word, intimate.

Batoni portrays Jesus offering his heart directly to the viewer. Jesus's anatomically correct heart, adorned at its top with a cross and a flame, is held aloft in his left hand, while the wound-scarred, upturned palm of his right hand is extended in a gesture inviting the viewer into relationship with him. His face is astonishingly beautiful. He is clearly a man, but his expression is open and unguarded to a degree that we rarely see in anyone, man or woman. Batoni gives Jesus the gaze and body language of a suitor proffering an engagement ring, except that instead of a ring, he is handing over nothing less than his heart.

I knelt before the painting, struck by how it was both familiar and, at the same time, novel. It was not my first time seeing it; I had visited Rome a handful of times previously and had made a point of seeing Batoni's *Sacred Heart* each time. I even have a large reproduction of it in my apartment, salvaged from the giveaway counter at the back of my parish church. But the painting itself has an almost unearthly beauty that no reproduction can fully capture, a beauty enhanced by the subdued lighting and sienna-colored marble walls that imbue the chapel with an almost womblike aura.

Although I was not expecting to receive a gift, there was one wished-for blessing I was hoping to receive—namely, the feeling of being touched by Jesus's Sacred Heart. To my surprise, as I knelt gazing at the painting, I did feel something.

Something lovely.

It wasn't exactly love so much as it was an *offer* of love.

What I felt was Jesus's vulnerability.

The word "vulnerability" comes from the Latin word for wound, *vulnus*. It literally means "woundability." As I spent a few moments with the Batoni image, Jesus seemed to be inviting me to contemplate his vulnerability—and my own as well.

I began to wonder: What am I really feeling sad about when I seek Jesus's love and don't feel it? I realized that I'm sad because I'm left to face my feelings of woundedness when what I really want is for Jesus to rescue me from those feelings. After all, isn't the Christian supposed to look to Jesus for consolation, for joy? Isn't that the whole point of devotion to the Sacred Heart—to accept Jesus at his word when he says, "Come to me, all you who labor and are burdened, and I will give you rest" (Matthew 11:28)?

Then I began to wonder how the devotion had come to play such an important role in the life of the church. I decided to use my skills as a rock-and-roll journalist to answer that question.

During the 1990s, record labels reissuing music by artists such as Harry Nilsson, Lesley Gore, and Del Shannon hired me to interview the artists and tell their life stories in the liner-note booklets that came with their compact discs. After I became Catholic and started broadcasting my faith in my blog, *The Dawn Patrol,* a reader derisively commented that I had shifted my loyalties from writing about rock artists to writing about saints. Although he meant it as an insult, he was right. I would always love the oldies, but the Catholic saints had become every bit as fascinating to me as the rockers who had engaged my imagination in my previous career.

And so, I set about getting to know the Sacred Heart in the same way I once got to know the songwriters and performers I wrote about. When covering the life and work of a rocker, if I really wanted to convey his or her personality to my readers, I didn't merely get to know the artists. I also acquainted myself with their friends, who, having seen sides of them I could never witness, could give me a fuller perspective.

In the case of the Sacred Heart of Jesus, the friends of Jesus's heart are the saints—not only canonized saints but also other holy people whose lives tell of their deep love for him (and his for them). When I study the saints' different expressions of devotion to the Sacred Heart, I gain a wider understanding of what friendship with Jesus looks like. That in turn helps me equip and, where necessary, reshape myself to be a better friend to him.

But hold on just one moment, you might be saying. *How did we get from the topic of devotion to the Sacred Heart to a more general discussion of friendship with Jesus? Could this be a devious attempt to avoid traditional piety in favor of a vague, watered-down, lowest-common-denominator approach to Catholic spirituality?*

Not at all! I don't believe discussion of friendship with Jesus takes us away at all from what is intended by Catholic forms of devotion to the Sacred Heart—and neither, for that matter, did that great champion of the devotion, Pope Pius XII, who wasn't exactly a mushy modernist. Pius emphasized that the various practices the church recommends to honor the Sacred Heart are not ends in themselves. They are useful only inasmuch as they bring us to both love Jesus more intensely and want to unite our personal offerings—our prayers, joys, works, and sufferings—to the saving offering that he accomplished for us on the cross.[1] The *Catechism of the Catholic Church* likewise stresses that devotion to the Sacred Heart comes down to reflecting upon how "Jesus knew and loved us each and all during his life, his agony and his Passion, and gave himself up for each one of us."[2]

Given that devotion to the Sacred Heart is really devotion to the love of Jesus, it is not surprising to find that it has been practiced in one form or another since the earliest days of the church. If we look for its origin, we will find that the scriptural foundation of the devotion to the Sacred Heart appears in the writings of St. John, the Beloved Disciple, which is why chapter one of this book explores John's contribution to the church's understanding of the Heart of Jesus. John's Gospel is especially important in the history of the devotion because it is the only Gospel that records that Jesus's heart was pierced by the lance of a centurion immediately after he expired on the cross.

After the apostolic age, during the era of the church fathers, St. Augustine became an important transitional figure in the history of the Sacred Heart devotion. His intensely personal writings

---

1. See Pius XII, Encyclical Letter *Haurietis aquas* (*On Devotion to the Sacred Heart*), §§112, 36, https://www.vatican.va/content/pius-xii/en/encyclicals/documents/hf_p-xii_enc_15051956_haurietis-aquas.html. I discuss that encyclical in detail in chapter five.

2. *Catechism of the Catholic Church*, 2nd ed. (Libreria Editrice Vaticana, 1997), §478, http://www.vatican.va/archive/ENG0015/_INDEX.HTM.

about prayer, which I explore in chapter two, gave voice to the desire of every Christian to take Jesus up on his offer to find rest in his loving heart (Matthew 11:28–30).

The spirituality of the Sacred Heart continued to develop during the Middle Ages with the help of monks and mystics. In chapter three, I mention some of the holy people from that era who brought the church to a deeper understanding of the devotion, including St. Bernard of Clairvaux as well as St. Lutgarde, a nun credited as the first saint to report receiving a vision of Jesus's pierced heart. Although the seventeenth-century French priest St. John Eudes deserves mention as the first to gain permission to celebrate a Mass honoring the Sacred Heart of Jesus, I have chosen to center chapter three upon a nun of his time who became wholly identified with the devotion: St. Margaret Mary Alacoque.

A member of the Order of the Visitation of Holy Mary, Sister Margaret Mary reported stunning visions in which Jesus asked the church to establish a Feast of the Sacred Heart. Aided by her spiritual director, St. Claude La Colombière, SJ, she ultimately succeeded in winning over her own religious institute to the devotion, which quickly spread throughout Europe and beyond. However, although the Holy See gave its approval to various local requests for celebrations of the Sacred Heart feast, it was reluctant to impose a new feast upon the universal church.

Finally, in 1856—more than 160 years after the death of St. Margaret Mary—the Holy See recognized that Catholic faithful around the world wanted to see the fulfillment of the desire that Jesus was said to have expressed for the feast. And so, Pope Pius IX decreed that the Feast of the Sacred Heart be added to the liturgical calendar worldwide. Pius IX's decree ushered in what could be called the golden age of devotion to the Sacred Heart. Over the following century, subsequent popes would place their own stamp upon the devotion, including Leo XIII, Pius XI, and Pius XII (the subject of chapter five), each of whom issued an encyclical recommending it to all the faithful. The church urged individuals and families to consecrate themselves. Popes consecrated nations and even, in the case of Leo XIII, the entire human race to the Sacred Heart.

During the 1930s, when devotion to the Sacred Heart was at its peak, the visions of St. Margaret Mary found an echo—one might even say a completion—in those of a Polish nun, St. Faustina Kowalska, who is the subject of chapter four. Perhaps more than any other saint, Faustina impresses upon me the extent to which, over the past two millennia, the Holy Spirit has been trying to tell us the same thing in different ways through different saints, tailoring its message to the particular needs of every age.

Also during the early part of the twentieth century, on the other side of the ocean from St. Faustina, that same Spirit moved Julia Greeley, a formerly enslaved African American woman, to bring the love of the Sacred Heart to a racially segregated city. Julia's story, which I explore in chapter six, and her personality touch me on a level that few others do.

Love of the Sacred Heart also motivated the twentieth-century married couple Catherine de Hueck and Eddie Doherty to accomplish extraordinary things while making extraordinary sacrifices. I chose to write about this remarkable pair in chapter seven because their lives illustrate two fundamental aspects of devotion to the Sacred Heart: nuptiality (being espoused to Jesus on a soul level) and sacrifice (making a gift of self to God through Jesus).

Although we may not all have visions of being mystically wed to Jesus, as did St. Margaret Mary and St. Faustina, every Christian is united to Jesus in the most intimate way possible by means of their baptism. This experience of loving union with Jesus, which the Catholic person experiences most dramatically through the Eucharist, has inspired saints throughout the ages to make extraordinary sacrifices in his name. At the start of chapter seven and as a prelude to Catherine and Eddie's story, I tell of two such self-sacrificing saints, the Roman martyr St. Tarcisius and the medieval religious sister St. Juliana Falconieri.

Father Pedro Arrupe, SJ's story in chapter eight seems a fitting place to close our explorations, as his life shows how devotion to the Sacred Heart can keep faith alive in the depths of suffering. I am also touched by the creativity and persistence he exhibited as he insisted upon the devotion's relevance at a time when many were arguing it should be consigned to the era of altar rails and fiddleback vestments.[3]

As this book goes to press, Pope Francis has issued an encyclical initiating a new chapter in the history of devotion to the Sacred Heart. I am grateful to have written here of many people whose writings and witness Francis highlights in *Dilexit nos*,[4]

---

3. I confess fondness for both altar rails and fiddleback vestments, though I'm glad to live in an era when I can make the responses at Mass out loud without people looking at me sideways.

4. Pope Francis, *Dilexit nos* (On the human and divine love of our Lord Jesus Christ), https://www.vatican.va/content/francesco/en/encyclicals/documents/20241024-enciclica-dilexit-nos.html.

including St. John, St. Augustine, St. Margaret Mary Alacoque, St. Thérèse of Lisieux, St. Faustina Kowalska, and Father Pedro Arrupe, SJ.

I am also grateful to have dedicated chapter five to Pius XII's *Haurietis aquas*, for Francis's encyclical cites it more than any other work except the Bible. As I note in that chapter, both Francis and Pius, while acknowledging the reality of sin, exhort the faithful to trust in God's abundant mercy. Francis places that mercy in a profoundly beautiful light as he assures us that we who are wounded by sin can have confidence in the compassion of Jesus, whose "risen heart preserves its wound as a constant memory."[5]

What I have learned from studying the saints' devotion to the Sacred Heart for this book leads me back to the Batoni image and the desire that it sparks in me to feel a joy that is not yet present. I do believe that Jesus wants me to look to him for joy. He has given me joys in this life, and I trust that he is not through doing so, even as I realize that such joys are only a foretaste of those that he wishes me to share with him in heaven. But contemplating the Batoni image of the Sacred Heart and the spirituality behind it helps me understand that my acute awareness of my vulnerability, and my longing to feel Jesus's nearness and love, do not constitute the cross that I sometimes think they do. Yes, they seemingly throw me back upon my own resources. But they are also a gift. They are a gift that Jesus is offering me so that I might make more space in my heart for him to fill.[6]

---

5. Francis, *Dilexit nos*, §155.

6. That is why I connect Augustine's writings on prayer with the Sacred Heart, as I write in chapter two.

As you read this book, my prayer is that, whatever you may feel or not feel, you will discover that, in the words Lucia of Fatima reported hearing from an angel, "the Hearts of Jesus and Mary are attentive to your supplications."[7] For wherever you find the Heart of Jesus, you will find the heart of his mother as well, and you will find both Jesus and Mary where I found them: in the heart of the church.

---

7. Donal Anthony Foley, *Marian Apparitions, the Bible, and the Modern World* (Eastbourne, UK: Gracewing, 2002), 232.

Chapter One

The Heart of a Beloved Disciple

St. John

St. Augustine once observed that St. John the Evangelist "said many things, and nearly everything was about love."[1]

John was able to write authoritatively about love because he listened to Jesus's Sacred Heart. His Gospel conveys this in the most literal way possible, as the apostle describes how, at the Last Supper, he "leaned back against Jesus's chest" (John 13:25). Among the eyewitnesses who wrote the Gospels, John is the only one who tells us he was so close to Jesus that he could hear the Savior's heartbeat. It was the consolation he received from his closeness to Jesus that gave him the confidence to call himself "the disciple whom Jesus loved" (John 21:7).

---

1. Augustine, *Homilies on the First Epistle of John*, trans. Boniface Ramsey (Hyde Park, NY: New City Press, 1990), 19. Translation amended; Ramsey has "charity" for Augustine's "caritas," which I have simplified to "love."

The real meaning of Jesus's Sacred Heart is found not in his physical organ but rather in the love with which he willed to take on a human nature to redeem us. In the same way, the real evidence that John listened to Jesus's heart is that he sought to emulate Jesus's love. Here are a few key ways in which the Gospels tell us that John was attentive to the desires of Jesus's heart:

- When Jesus first called John along with his brother James, John immediately left behind his old life and all he possessed to follow Jesus (Matthew 4:18–22; Mark 1:16–20; Luke 5:1–11).
- John continued to follow Jesus even after Jesus rebuked him for his desire for revenge against the Samaritan village that refused to welcome Jesus (Luke 9:51–56).
- John remained with Jesus even after many other disciples, scandalized by Jesus's Bread of Life discourse, "returned to their former way of life" (John 6:66).
- When John, in presenting his personal wants to Jesus, failed to receive an outright yes or no answer (Mark 10:35–40), he continued to follow Jesus, trusting in his will.
- John was the only disciple willing to risk opprobrium by remaining with Jesus during the Crucifixion (John 19:26).
- John accepted without question Jesus's dying wish that he receive Mary as his own mother (John 19:26; admittedly, that was not so much a burden to be assumed as it was an invaluable gift).

- John honored the leadership of Peter, whom Jesus had made head of the twelve apostles (Matthew 16:18), by letting Peter be the first apostle to witness the empty tomb, even though John arrived first (John 20:1–9).
- John maintained faith in Jesus for the rest of his life, trusting in the goodness of Jesus's will, even after the risen Jesus refused to grant him insight into what his future might hold (John 21:20–23).

We also know from John's letters that the Beloved Disciple continued to listen to Jesus's heart, and that he urged others to do the same. It is traditionally believed that John continued to witness Jesus's love with every last bit of energy he had. As St. Jerome relates:

> The blessed John the Evangelist lived in Ephesus until extreme old age. His disciples could barely carry him to church and he could not muster the voice to speak many words. During individual gatherings he usually said nothing but, "Little children, love one another." The disciples and brothers in attendance, annoyed because they always heard the same words, finally said, "Teacher, why do you always say this?" He replied with a line worthy of John: "Because it is the Lord's commandment and if it alone is kept, it is sufficient."[2]

I have to smile at this evidence that complaints about short, repetitive homilies date all the way back to apostolic times. But if we accept the anecdote as authentic—and there is no reason not

---

2. Jerome, *Commentary on Galatians*, trans. Andrew Cain (Washington: Catholic University of America Press, 2010), 260.

to do so, given its consistency with John's writings—it conveys the most concise theology of the Sacred Heart, namely, that Jesus Christ, our Lord, who loves us from the depths of his heart, wills that we love one another so we may share in the redemption that he has won for us on the cross.

There is another important way in which John, in his Gospel, teaches us about the love of the Sacred Heart: through his accounts of two events in the life of Jesus that do not appear in the other Gospels. Both accounts concern wondrous events that John personally witnessed—and they are related.

The first of these events is the miracle Jesus performed at the wedding at Cana (John 2:1–11) when, by changing water into wine, he presaged how, through his Passion, death, and Resurrection, he would offer his own Body and Blood "for the life of the world" (John 6:51). The second is the account of how blood and water poured from Jesus's Sacred Heart after he had died, when a centurion pierced his side with a lance (John 19:34).

Many church authors call the flow of blood and water a miracle in and of itself, as dead bodies do not normally bleed, and the separate flow of water is unheard of. However, the church does not officially call it a miracle, and various medical explanations are often proposed to explain the unusual physiological response. Whatever one chooses to think (I cast my vote for "miraculous"), church fathers and other theological authorities agree that the blood and water from Jesus's side is *wondrous*. That is to say, it is a mystery of Jesus's Passion that should inspire us to pause a moment and reflect with reverence, just as John himself invites us to do (John 19:35–37).

What, then, is the connection between these two seemingly disparate wonders, that of the miracle at Cana and that of the blood and water? For one thing, the wedding at Cana is the Gospel's first account of Jesus performing a miraculous sign that demonstrated his divinity, whereas the blood and water is, in a sense, his final sign—at least, the final one before his Resurrection. For another, Jesus's mother Mary is present at both events—a sign of the profound union of hearts between mother and son.

But there are also less obvious connections between Jesus's miracle at Cana and the wondrous flow of blood and water from his Sacred Heart. I would like to take a moment to delve into them, because understanding the relationship between these two wonders can provide a profound preparation for understanding how various saints have understood the heart of Jesus.

When Jesus changes water into wine at Cana, it is a symbol of joy, which John affirms by telling us the headwaiter pronounced it "good wine" (John 2:10). Jesus is, in effect, giving his blessing to the joyful occasion where (with a nudge from Mary) he chose to perform the miracle: a wedding. But whose wedding is it? John's Gospel doesn't say—and, from the time of the earliest commentaries on John, the church has believed there is a reason for that. The miracle is Jesus's way of saying that he himself is the true bridegroom. He loves his bride, the church, so much that he will "[hand] himself over for her to sanctify her" (Ephesians 5:25–26). In the words of Augustine:

The Lord, as an invited guest, came to the wedding. What is surprising if the one who came into this world for a wedding went to that house for a wedding? . . . The Lord has a bride here [in this world] whom he redeemed with his blood, and to whom he gave the pledge of the Holy Spirit. He snatched her from bondage to the devil, he died for her transgressions, he rose again for her justification.[3]

It may feel strange or even uncomfortable to think of Jesus as our bridegroom. When I try to understand it, I remember that, although mystics tell of experiencing Christ as the spouse of their soul, all that we need for salvation is to understand Jesus as sacred Scripture describes him. And when we look to see how the Bible describes Jesus as bridegroom, we find that it always—and only—describes him as bridegroom of the entire church, not of the individual, except inasmuch as the individual is part of the church. In this way, sacred Scripture reveals Jesus as the fulfillment of the prophecies God gave the people of ancient Israel when he promised to grant children to the formerly deserted and barren wife (see Isaiah 54:1):

For your husband is your Maker;
the LORD of hosts is his name,
Your redeemer, the Holy One of Israel,
called God of all the earth. (Isaiah 54:5)

In the New Testament, the once "barren wife" of Isaiah 54, who now rejoices in being united in marriage to her divine Redeemer, is shown to be the "Jerusalem above . . . and she is our mother" (Galatians

---

3. Augustine, Homily 8 §4, in *Homilies on the Gospel of John*, ed. Allan D. Fitzgerald and trans. Edmund Hill (Hyde Park, NY: New City Press, 2009), 171. "He died for her transgressions; he rose again for her justification" is a reference to Romans 4:25.

4:26)—that is, Holy Mother Church.[4] The fifth-century church father Cyril of Alexandria, reflecting upon Isaiah's description of God as Israel's maker and husband, preached that God, in espousing the church to himself through Jesus Christ in the Holy Spirit,

> is making you rather than creating you, transferring us into another type of citizenship and beautiful life. For we are being transformed in Christ into the newness of the holy and evangelical life, according to his own beautiful form through the Spirit so that others see us as different from the rest [of humanity].[5]

We can see, then, that the intent of Scripture in pointing to Jesus as the bridegroom of the church is not to reduce him to the level of a human husband, and it is certainly not to project human sexual desire upon him.[6] Rather, the Bible seeks to impress upon

---

4. See also Hebrews 12:22 and Revelation 21:2.

5. Cyril of Alexandria, "Isaiah 40-66" in *Ancient Christian Commentary on Scripture, Old Testament, vol. 11*, ed. Mark W. Elliot (Downers Grove, IL: IVP Academic, 2007), 170. With his references to being "transformed in Christ" into newness of life, Cyril draws upon Romans 6:4 and 12:2.

6. In making this distinction, it is important to emphasize that Jesus, through his Passion, death, and Resurrection, has redeemed human nature in its entirety, including human sexuality. Due to the concupiscence that remains in the human person even after baptism (*Catechism of the Catholic Church*, §2520), Christians are not exempt from the struggle necessary to practice virtue and self-control in the sexual sphere (as in every area of life), but they can trust that God's grace is available to assist them. For more on how the church calls every person to live the virtue of chastity according to their state of life (that is, whether they are single or married), see Fulton J. Sheen, *Three to Get Married* (Princeton, NJ: Appleton-Century-Crofts Inc., 1951; repr., Scepter Pubs., 2004); Pope Benedict XVI, Encyclical Letter *Deus caritas est* (*God Is Love*), December 25, 2005, https://www.vatican.va/content/benedict-xvi/en/encyclicals/documents/hf_ben-xvi_enc_20051225_deus-caritas-est.html; and Pope Francis, Post-Synodal Apostolic Exhortation *Amoris laetitia* (*The Joy of Love*), March 19, 2016, https://www.vatican.va/content/francesco/en/apost_exhortations/documents/papa-francesco_esortazione-ap_20160319_amoris-laetitia.html.

us that Jesus, taking on human nature, descends from heaven to unite himself to the church so he may transform it through his divine nature and raise it with him to heaven. The Cana miracle is a beautiful illustration of this transformation that Jesus desires to effect upon the church as a whole and upon every one of us in particular—a transformation that he will set into motion when he enters into his Passion.

With that in mind, we are now able to understand the deepest level of connection between the Cana miracle and the outpouring of blood and water from Jesus's wounded heart following his death upon the cross. Just as the transformation of the water into wine at Cana points to Jesus's Passion, so too does the flow of blood and water point to the birth of the church that will soon be made manifest when God bestows the Holy Spirit at Pentecost (Acts 2:2–41).[7] The *Catechism* puts it succinctly: "The Church is born primarily of Christ's total self-giving for our salvation."[8]

---

7. This interpretation dates from the early centuries of the church and is cited in two documents of the Second Vatican Council, *Sacrosanctum concilium*, §5, https://www.vatican.va/archive/hist_councils/ii_vatican_council/documents/vat-ii_const_19631204_sacrosanctum-concilium_en.html; and *Lumen gentium*, §3, https://www.vatican.va/archive/hist_councils/ii_vatican_council/documents/vat-ii_const_19641121_lumen-gentium_en.html.

8. *Catechism*, §766.

Nowhere is Jesus's total self-giving more evident than in his death on the cross. It is there that he demonstrates most fully how "he loved his own in the world and he loved them to the end" (John 13:1). The blood and water from his side, in representing the birth of the church, thus reveal the loving plan that God had from "the beginning" (Genesis 1:1) to re-create and unite "all things in Christ, in heaven and on earth" (Ephesians 1:10). In the *Catechism*, this connection between creation and redemption is beautifully expressed in a passage drawn from the teachings of St. Ambrose, the bishop who mentored St. Augustine: "As Eve was formed from the sleeping Adam's side, so the Church was born from the pierced heart of Christ hanging dead on the cross."[9]

During Jesus's earthly life, his body radiated healing power for those who approached him in faith (see Luke 6:19). Just as the wondrous flow of blood and water represents the church that Jesus creates through pouring himself out, it also represents the means that Jesus has chosen so that, acting through the church, he might bring his healing power to people in every age: the sacraments. From the earliest days of the church, commentators have understood the blood and water to represent the Eucharist and Baptism, the principal sacraments from which the power of the other sacraments flow.[10]

A key quality of people who love each other—whether they are friends, family members, or spouses—is their desire to communicate with each other about their hopes, dreams, and plans for the future. John, the Beloved Disciple, in listening to Jesus's

---

9. *Catechism*, §766.

10. See *Catechism*, §1116; Thomas Aquinas, *Summa Theologiae* 3.62.5

Sacred Heart, came as close as anyone can in this life to understanding Jesus's ultimate hopes, dreams, and plans for him and all of humanity. He learned that, through Jesus's Sacred Heart, God loved the human race with the same Holy Spirit love with which the Father and Jesus loved one another before the foundation of the world (see John 17:23-24). And he learned that God intended that Jesus, through his Sacred Heart, would continue to pour out his love through the church and its sacraments until his return (see John 14:3).

In short, through John's Gospel, we come to understand that when we listen to the Heart of Jesus, we find that we ourselves are beloved disciples—for, to borrow a thought from another John, church father St. John Chrysostom, God loves each of us as though there were only one of us.[11]

---

11. "[God] has the same love for every individual as for the whole world." John Chrysostom, quoted in *Galatians, Ephesians, Philippians: New Testament Vol. 8*, Ancient Christian Commentary on Scripture, ed. Mark J. Edwards (Downers Grove, IL: IVP Academic, 1999), 32.

Chapter Two

The Restless Heart
St. Augustine

In 1960, hundreds of thousands of pop-music fans purchased Connie Francis's hit single "My Heart Has a Mind of Its Own"— few knowing that the song's title metaphor was perfected more than fifteen hundred years earlier by a North African saint.

St. Augustine, the bishop of the ancient Roman city of Hippo (in what is now Algeria), who died in 430, often warns of the dangers of having a heart with a mind of its own. "[God] is very close to the heart, but the heart has wandered from him," he writes in his iconic memoir *Confessions*. "'Return, sinners, to your heart,' and adhere to him who made you."[1]

But Augustine isn't content with giving the heart only a mind of its own. The 200 or so references to the heart in *Confessions* include references to "the ears of [the] heart," "the

---

1. Augustine, *Confessions,* trans. Henry Chadwick (New York: Oxford University Press, 1998), 63. The quotation within the quote is from the Septuagint translation of Isaiah 46:8.

mouth of the heart," and even "the hand of [the] heart."[2] And yes, in many of his other writings, Augustine does refer to the "eyes of the heart" (though for some reason he refrained from giving the heart a nose).[3]

We might even say that Augustine imagines the heart with legs or even wings, for in what is perhaps the most famous quote of his *Confessions*, in its very first paragraph, he cries out to God: "You have made us for yourself, and our heart is restless until it rests in you."[4]

Augustine's exclamation professing his intensely "restless" longing for union with God retains its power to stun. We don't often see Christian faith portrayed in terms of dissatisfaction. Many popular preachers promote a kind of prosperity gospel, selling Christianity as though it were a product that, if purchased (through large donations to the preachers' churches), would surely bring fulfillment and even monetary gain in this life. However, to borrow an expression from Dietrich Bonhoeffer, the Lutheran pastor martyred by the Nazis for his work in the German resistance movement during World War II, such "cheap grace" is far from the authentic gospel.[5]

With that said, because we are so used to having Christianity sold to us as a kind of cure-all, if we read Augustine's words too quickly, we might assume the saint is simply attesting that,

---

2. Augustine, *Confessions*, 5, 171, and 185.

3. These observations are drawn from a search of the Latin database of Augustine's writings on the Sant'Agostino website, augustinus.it.

4. Augustine, *Confessions*, 3.

5. See Dietrich Bonhoeffer, *The Cost of Discipleship* (New York: Touchstone, 1995), chapter one.

although he once was restless, he now reposes in God. But the ensuing pages of his *Confessions* forestall such a pat interpretation. Just a few paragraphs after speaking of how our heart is restless until it rests in God, Augustine begs God to speak to him. "See," he pleads, "the ears of my heart are before you. Open them and 'say to my soul, I am your salvation' [Psalms 35:3]."

"After that utterance," Augustine adds, "I will run and lay hold on you."

With those words, Augustine effectively affirms that he, like St. Paul (who often likened faith to running the good race),[6] holds that the Christian's life on earth is a life in motion. We do yet rest in God, in the sense that, having found him, we seek no other. But when we reflect upon our encounter with him, we long to get closer. Like C.S. Lewis's cry to go "further up and further in,"[7] we find that if we remain where we are, we risk Christ's passing us by. We need rather to call after Jesus like the blind man in Luke's gospel who, when he heard that Christ was close at hand, insistently cried out until Jesus invited him to draw near (Luke 18:35–43).

To Augustine, as with all the saints, there can be no sideways movement in the spiritual life—only growth or backsliding. (As Jesuit Father Daniel A. Lord, SJ, put it, "Grow! When you stop growing spiritually, you are asleep or dead.")[8] In his continuing desire to "run and lay hold of" God, Augustine therefore seeks to attune his heart—and its figurative eyes, ears, mouth, hand,

---

6. See, for example, 1 Corinthians 9:24–27.

7. C.S. Lewis, *The Last Battle* (London: Collins, 2003), 162.

8. Thomas F. Gavin, *Champion of Youth: A Dynamic Story of a Dynamic Man, Daniel A. Lord, SJ* (Boston: St. Paul Editions, 1977), 198.

legs, and wings[9]—to the heart of Christ. He accomplishes this attunement in innumerable ways, from reading sacred Scripture to living virtuously and practicing acts of mercy. But one indispensable activity underlies all he does to make his heart like that of Jesus: the constant work of prayer.

I say that Augustine's work of prayer is constant because he strives to follow St. Paul's dictum to "pray without ceasing." But that raises the question: How is it humanly possible to pray without ceasing? Thankfully, Augustine gives us a masterly answer to that question with an epistle on prayer, known as Letter 130, that remains as relevant for Christian readers today as it was when he composed it in the early fifth century.

Actually, with Letter 130, Augustine answers not just one but a multitude of questions—most notably why we should bother to pray at all, given that God already knows our desires. If we examine it closely, searching especially for guidance on how to bring our prayers in closer union with the desires of the heart of Christ, we will find that the letter is as interesting for a question that it doesn't resolve as it is for the many questions it does.

Augustine frames Letter 130 as a personal letter to Proba, a pious widow who, when the Goths invaded Rome in 410, had fled to North Africa with her daughter-in-law Juliana (also a widow)

---

9. And also its voice; see *Confessions*, 213. With that, I shall cease enumerating the various bodily characteristics of Augustine's heart.

and granddaughter Demetrias. But in fact, he intends that the letter be read by anyone interested in prayer. Proba simply posed the question—how to pray without ceasing—that prompted him to write. We, in reading his words, thus can and even should take them to be addressed personally to us.

The Bishop of Hippo begins by praising Proba for her desire to ask him about prayer, given that she is a wealthy woman. He notes that her question shows that, in keeping with St. Paul's advice to the rich, she looks to God for security rather than to her wealth, for her heart is set not on riches but on the "true life" of heaven (1 Timothy 6:17–19).[10] The saint then urges Proba to follow Paul's line of thinking all the way to its conclusion: "Out of a love for this true life, therefore, you should also regard yourself as desolate in this world, however great the happiness with which you are living in it."

In recommending a "desolate" perspective, Augustine is not glorifying the kind of desolation that spiritual directors typically (and rightly) urge their directees to guard against. His point is not that Christians should condemn themselves to a life of depression. Rather, Augustine seeks to demonstrate that the Christian, in order to thrive, needs to have a right scale of values. Having a right scale of values requires recognizing that not all good things bring the same quality of happiness. Augustine observes, for example, that the quality of happiness that wealth brings is not at the same level as that which a good friend brings. Even the happiness we receive from friendship has its limits, he notes, for "where

---

10. All quotations from Augustine's Letter 130 are taken from Augustine, *Letters 100-155*, ed. Boniface Ramsey, trans. Roland Teske (Hyde Park, NY: New City Press, 2003).

is such a friend found about whose heart and character one can in this life have a certain confidence?" Since we long to be happy, but are incapable of knowing true happiness until our union with Christ is fulfilled in the true life of heaven, Augustine writes, "the Christian soul ought to regard itself as desolate so that it does not cease to pray."

As Augustine writes about the "true life," it becomes clear that, in the back of his mind, he associates it with the "true light" that St. John speaks of (John 1:9). He makes the connection explicit when he adds that the Christian soul that prays without ceasing will look to sacred Scripture "as if to a lamp set in a dark place"—a lamp taking its source from "the light shines in the darkness, and the darkness has not overcome it" (John 1:5).

Although in this life we can glimpse the ineffable true light through reading the Bible, in the true life of heaven we will be able to see it clearly. But "in order to see it," Augustine writes, "hearts must be cleansed by faith." With those words, the saint telegraphs that the true intent of his letter is to outline his theology of the heart—which we could also call his theology of desire.

Augustine brings his theology of the heart into focus when he addresses the question of why Jesus says "ask and it will be given to you" (Matthew 7:7), given that our desires are already known to God. The question, he writes, "can trouble the mind unless we understand that the Lord our God does not want our will, which he cannot fail to know, to become known to him, but our desire, by which we can receive what he prepares to give, to be exercised in prayers."

The operative word in Augustine's answer is "exercised." If, as the poet James Weldon wrote, "your arm's too short to box with God,"[11] so too, on Augustine's account, our heart is too small to contain God. And (sticking with athletic metaphors for the moment), just as acrobats practice stretching their muscles so they can leap great distances, so too Augustine wants us to practice stretching our desire. With prayer as our spiritual exercise, our heart is open wide.

And so, Augustine writes, our ability to receive the true life that God is preparing to give us depends upon how much "we believe it with more fidelity, and hope for it more firmly, and love it more ardently." Therefore, he adds, we "always pray with a continuous desire filled with faith, hope, and love." On this understanding, Paul's exhortation to "pray without ceasing" means "'desire without ceasing the happy life'—which is none but eternal life, and desire it from him who alone can give it."

I am trying to avoid projecting upon Augustine the kind of pious expressions of devotion to the Sacred Heart of Jesus that would not even begin to emerge in the church for another millennium. But it is hard not to see in his words the implication that when we desire God in everything we do throughout our daily life, we form our heart so that it is more like God's own heart—to which we have access through the heart of Jesus. He seems to say

---

11. James Weldon Johnson, "The Prodigal Son," in *Complete Poems* (New York: Penguin Books, 2000), 18.

as much when he writes of the union of love that ensues when, in our desire for God, we set aside time in our day specifically for prayer.

Augustine's description of the human heart at prayer really does read like a love story. Prayer, he writes, need not consist only of words, for "much talking is one thing; a lasting love is another." Instead of relying upon words, we may instead "knock with a long and pious stirring of the heart." When he adds that our sighs and tears often express our desires better than our verbal pleadings, Augustine makes evident that, in his mind, the God to whom we pray is one who understands our human heart from the inside. He is presenting a spirituality of the Sacred Heart in everything but name.

Yet, however much God may hear the sighs and tears of the faithful, Augustine admits that vocal prayer still has its place. We "need words by which we may be reminded and may consider what we ask for," he writes, "not by which we believe that we should either instruct or persuade the Lord." That is to say, when we pray, the words we use should bring us to reflect upon what it is that we truly need and desire from God.

How may we be certain that, when we make vocal prayer, we are asking God to fulfill our genuine needs and not merely to give us what we humanly desire—which may or may not be God's will for us? The best way to be certain that our own petitions are wise,

Augustine writes, is to compare them with those of the Lord's Prayer, because everything God wants us to desire is contained within that prayer.

Augustine allows that we may express our desires to God in words that relate directly to our personal situation. For example, if I pray that, Lord willing, I might be accepted for the job that I applied for, Augustine would approve, for I am really saying, "Thy will be done. . . . Give us this day our daily bread." But he insists that "we should not to be free to make other petitions" besides those in the Lord's Prayer. Thus, he writes, if we are tempted to pray for wealth, power, or fame, we would be better off praying, "Deliver us from evil," in the hope that God would rid us of such worldly desires. The entire thrust of Letter 130, then, is to impress upon the reader that we don't pray to change God's will so that he may give us what we desire; rather, we pray to change our own will so that we may desire what God wants to give us. If we are praying rightly, we are asking the Lord unceasingly to enlarge our hearts—that is, our desires—and to unite them with the desires of his own Heart.

Yet, I cannot help but notice that Augustine adds a line toward the end of Letter 130 that seems to contradict the rest of the letter's message. "Remember, of course, to pray earnestly for us too," he tells Proba—and, in case that isn't clear enough, he adds, "we need the help of your sisterly prayers." Ordinarily I would expect a bishop to end a letter asking for prayers. But by the time Augustine makes his prayer request in Letter 130, he has just finished writing at length that we pray so that God may reshape our own desires. Why, then, would he "need the help" of Proba's prayers? The theology of prayer that he has just outlined simply doesn't seem to leave a place for intercessory prayer.

But I think I can find an answer—at least, a partial one—in another writing of Augustine's. In his *Expositions on the Psalms*, when writing on Psalm 62, he takes a fascinating detour to discuss Paul's intriguing words in Colossians 1:24: "Now I rejoice in my sufferings for your sake, and in my flesh I am filling up what is lacking in the afflictions of Christ on behalf of his body, which is the church."

Augustine understands the Colossians verse to mean that God has ordained that, over the course of history from Jesus's ascension until his return, the members of the Body of Christ are to add their sufferings to those of their head—that is, Christ. What is lacking in the afflictions of Christ, Augustine writes, are your and my own sufferings, as a member of Christ's Body living in this particular time and place:

> You suffer so much as was to be contributed out of your sufferings to the whole suffering of Christ, [who] suffered as our Head, and [now] suffers in His members, that is, in our own selves. Unto this our common republic, as it were each of us according to our measure pays that which we owe, and according to the powers which we have, as it were a quota of sufferings we contribute.[12]

---

12. Augustine, "Expositions on the Book of Psalms", in *A Select Library of the Nicene and Post-Nicene Fathers*, 1st ser., vol. 8, ed. Philip Schaff (Buffalo, NY: Christian Literature Publishing Co., 1888), 252. Translation modified. The Latin text was consulted, as was Maria Boulding's translation. See Maria Boulding, *Expositions of the Psalms, 51–72*, vol. 3, ed. John E. Rotelle, trans. and notes by Maria Boulding (Hyde Park, NY: New City Press, 1999), 204.

If we read Augustine's Letter 130 in light of this profound spirituality of suffering, we can see why he would attribute value to Proba's prayers for him. The more Proba follows Augustine's advice, praying in such a way that she unites her heart to the heart of Christ, the more closely she will be joined to Christ in everything she does—including her sufferings. And when she does suffer, Christ will add her afflictions to his own treasury of merit—the same treasury of merit that he draws upon to send his transforming and redeeming grace to those in need of it. In praying for Augustine, then, Proba is asking God to send him grace that she herself, with God's help, participated in acquiring.

That, at least, is why I think Augustine wants Proba's prayers. But he himself, as a gentle shepherd of souls, does not want her to suffer if such suffering could be avoided. In particular, knowing her obligations to her family members who depended upon her, Augustine does not want Proba to feel obliged to overexert herself in prayer.

"You, of course, owe an account of your conscience to God," Augustine writes in closing, "but you should owe no one anything except to love one another. May the Lord hear your prayer who is able to do more than what we ask for and understand." In this way, Augustine invites Proba, and all of us, to imitate Jesus, whose wounded heart does not remain closed upon itself, but instead opens up to embrace all who suffer.

Chapter Three

The Heart
Made Manifest

St. Margaret Mary Alacoque

If you were to search Catholic literature prior to the seventeenth century for the words "Sacred Heart," you would find few references. But appearances can be deceiving, for the Sacred Heart was very much on the minds of theologians, preachers, and mystics during the Middle Ages and early Renaissance—just not in so many words. Some of the best-known holy people of that time promoted what we would now call devotion to the Sacred Heart, or experienced a mystical union with the Heart of Jesus, including:[1]

---

1. The examples which follow are all drawn from Josef Stierli, "Devotion to the Sacred Heart from the End of Patristic Times down to St. Margaret Mary," in *Heart of the Saviour: A Symposium on Devotion to the Sacred Heart,* trans. Paul Andrews (New York: Herder & Herder, 1957).

- St. Bernard of Clairvaux, who, in his *Commentary on the Song of Songs*, rhapsodized about the "secret" of Jesus's heart.
- St. Bonaventure, who writes in his *Journey of the Mind to God* that the only way to God is through "the most burning love of Christ crucified."
- St. Gertrude the Great, a nun, mystic, and spiritual writer who prayed, "Dear Jesus, hide me in the wound of thy most loving Heart, away from all that is not thee."
- St. Albert the Great, best known as the mentor of St. Thomas Aquinas, who wrote of Jesus, "Why was he wounded on the side near his Heart? In order that we may never tire of contemplating his Heart."
- St. Peter Canisius, who, at the altar of the Blessed Sacrament at St. Peter's Basilica in Rome, received a vision in which Jesus displayed his heart and invited him to "drink the waters of salvation from that fountain."
- St. John Eudes, who in 1672 at the Grand Seminary of Rennes celebrated the first liturgical Feast of the Sacred Heart, having obtained his bishop's approval.[2]

Many more names could be added to these, including female mystics such as St. Lutgarde and St. Catherine of Siena, each of whom reported a vision in which Jesus granted her desire for a mystical exchange of her own heart for his.

What is particularly striking about the list above—and it is only a partial one—is that it includes important figures from nearly all the major religious orders of the medieval and

---

2. The feast that Eudes celebrated was approved only for his own diocese of Rennes, not for the universal church.

early Counter-Reformation-era church. Bernard and Lutgarde were Cistercians, Bonaventure was a Franciscan, Gertrude was a Benedictine,[3] Albert and Catherine were Dominicans, Peter Canisius was a Jesuit, and John Eudes was the founder of the Eudists. It would seem as though the Holy Spirit was working within the church to prepare the hearts of the faithful for the formal devotion to the Sacred Heart when it arose.

Given that so many great Catholics were already speaking of Jesus's heart prior to the time of St. Margaret Mary Alacoque, including many doctors of the church,[4] we might well ask why Margaret Mary, a seventeenth-century Visitation nun, is credited with originating the Sacred Heart devotion. The short answer is that she received private revelations that both confirmed what others had said about the devotion and provided a profound new way of understanding what God wished to accomplish with it. In addition, unlike previous visionaries, Margaret Mary reported receiving a request from Jesus for liturgical recognition of the devotion, along with promises for those who practiced the devotion.

Taken together, the theological insights that St. Margaret Mary received, along with the request for liturgical recognition of the Sacred Heart and the accompanying promises, amounted to

---

3. Some authorities call Gertrude a Cistercian, as her monastery followed the Cistercian tradition; in any case, the Cistercians grew out of the Benedictine order.

4. The title of doctor of the church (*doctor* being meant in the Latin sense of *teacher*) is granted by the pope to saints whose writings, preaching, or sayings, as well as their way of life, bear witness to the faith in a manner that lends high authority to their teachings.

marching orders for the church—a divinely ordained to-do list. In a way, the truly extraordinary thing is not so much that Jesus appeared to Margaret Mary but rather that the highest level of the church was willing to listen to her private revelations and grant them official approval. Then, as now, the desires of a single cloistered nun, even one who claims she is reporting the express will of Jesus, don't normally lead the Holy See to promote a devotion, let alone to establish a feast for the universal church.

Before we explore the most momentous content of St. Margaret Mary's revelations, it is worth taking a moment to look at Catholic teaching on private revelations in general. The *Catechism of the Catholic Church* explains that, unlike the public revelation that God gave through sacred Scripture and the event of the Incarnation that Scripture describes, private revelations that have been approved by the church "do not belong . . . to the deposit of faith. It is not their role to improve or complete Christ's definitive Revelation, but to help live more fully by it in a certain period of history."[5] The church, in approving a private revelation, therefore does nothing more than propose it for belief. No Catholic is required to believe a private revelation, even an approved one. As Cardinal Joseph Ratzinger, the future Pope Benedict XVI, wrote when commenting on the Third Secret of Fatima, such revelations are "a help which is offered, but which one is not obliged to use."[6] I find Ratzinger's words reassuring because, to be honest, there are aspects of approved private

---

5. *Catechism*, §67.

6. Joseph Ratzinger, "Theological Commentary," in "Documents regarding 'The Message of Fatima,'" https://www.vatican.va/roman_curia/congregations/cfaith/documents/rc_con_cfaith_doc_20000626_message-fatima_en.html

revelations that I find difficult to take—particularly in the writings of St. Margaret Mary and her greatest spiritual heir, St. Faustina Kowalska (see chapter four).

As we will see, there are many similarities between St. Margaret Mary's experience of Jesus and that of St. Faustina. Each of them felt from a young age that God was calling her not only to enter the convent but also, in doing so, to share intimately in the sufferings that Jesus endured for the salvation of souls. And although each of them was what the church calls a "bride of Christ" through her religious vows, their experiences of their espousal to Jesus were unusually intense. He was as real to them as an earthly husband.

Margaret Mary's and Faustina's spiritual perceptions of Jesus are not unique in the annals of saints. Holy people naturally experience Christ's presence more intensely and more intimately than the rest of us. They are eager to accept opportunities to become more like him through acts of penance for sin. But, although I realize that I too am called to holiness (as is every human being),[7] I have trouble relating to the saints' description of Jesus as a husband who continually invites them to accept opportunities to suffer on his behalf, which they accept with joy. And I likewise have a hard time identifying with how eagerly they accept the invitation. I identify more with the character in a Flannery O'Connor story who "could never be a saint, but thought she could be a martyr if they killed her quick."[8]

---

7. *Catechism*, §2013.

8. Flannery O'Connor, *The Complete Stories* (New York: Farrar, Straus & Giroux, 1971), 243. The quotation is from O'Connor's story "A Temple of the Holy Ghost."

So I am comforted by the assurance the church gives me that its approval relates to the theological substance of the visions and not to whether the entirety of the "he said/she said" dialogue that the visionaries reported is accurate. Such assurance comes through the various popes who have promulgated documents or delivered talks in which they identify the aspects of Margaret Mary's and Faustina's revelations that are most important for our faith. In reflecting on Margaret Mary's contributions to the spirituality of the Sacred Heart, our guide will be the two great encyclicals on the Sacred Heart: Pius XI's *Miserentissimus Redemptor* (1928) and Pius XII's *Haurietis aquas* (1956).[9]

Although Margaret Mary Alacoque (1647–1690) was born into a well-to-do family in France's Burgundy region, her living circumstances turned dire after her father died when she was eight. Margaret Mary's father had willed his estate to an uncle who became her family's custodian. In the uncle's home, Margaret Mary, her mother, and her four brothers were treated worse than servants. Not only were they made to wait upon the uncle's family, they had to plead for their most basic needs.[10]

---

9. Because the content of *Haurietis aquas* is so rich, going well beyond St. Margaret Mary's revelations, we will look at it in depth in chapter five.

10. Unless otherwise noted, all biographical information on the saint is taken from her memoir: Margaret Mary Alacoque, *The Autobiography of St. Margaret Mary*, trans. Vincent Kerns (Westminster, MD: Newman Press, 1961).

Most of what we know about Margaret Mary's life comes from a memoir she composed at the request of a spiritual director after she made her vows in the convent. She wrote that God held a claim on her heart "from babyhood."[11] Even before she knew what perpetual chastity meant, she felt compelled inwardly to vow it at Mass during the consecration of the Eucharist. As she entered her teens and began to make her desire for a religious vocation known to her family, Margaret Mary encountered strong opposition from her relatives. "The family [was] urging me to get married," Margaret recalled, "mother, most of all; she never stopped crying; I was her only hope of getting away—once I was settled in a home of my own, she would be able to come and live with me."[12]

Various members of Margaret Mary's family tried over the next several years to manipulate and even threaten her into following their will for her life rather than her own. But eventually there came a time when Margaret Mary, by then twenty-three years old, felt strong enough to insist upon entering the convent where she felt certain God wanted her to be: the Visitation Monastery at Paray-le-Monial.

Margaret Mary gained a reputation at Paray for being prone to becoming completely absorbed in prayer. Her ecstasies, however, did not endear her to her superiors; rather, they caused concern. She was told to resist the temptation to lose herself in thoughts of God, and, as an obedient religious, she was pained at being unable to follow the command.[13]

---

11. Alacoque, *Autobiography*, 3.

12. Alacoque, *Autobiography*, 12.

13. We should not judge Margaret Mary's superiors too harshly for imagining she could prevent being overwhelmed by God's making himself present to her as she prayed. Holiness such as hers was unusual even within convent walls.

In ordinary conversation, we sometimes speak of someone "opening their heart" to us. For Margaret Mary, that is literally what Jesus did when he appeared to her while she was adoring the Blessed Sacrament on December 27, 1673—appropriately, the Feast of St. John, the Apostle of the Sacred Heart. In the first of her four major revelations of the Sacred Heart, the nun felt that Jesus was present, inviting her to rest her head upon his breast as did the Beloved Disciple at the Last Supper (John 13:23–25). At that moment, she wrote, "He revealed to me the wonders of his love and the inexplicable secrets of his Sacred Heart, which he had always withheld from me until he opened his Heart to me for the first time."[14] It seemed to Margaret Mary that Jesus then said:

> My divine Heart so passionately loves all people and you in particular that, no longer able to contain the flames of its burning charity, it has to pour them forth through you, and it must manifest itself to them, to enrich them with its precious treasures, which I am revealing to you, and which contain the sanctifying and salutary graces necessary to snatch them from the abyss of perdition.[15]

What strikes me immediately about these reported words of Jesus is the reference to "all people and you in particular." Margaret Mary's vision affirms what we know about Christ from the Gospels: when he extends his love to us, he is not merely loving some vague idea of humanity. In gazing upon us, he sees each and every one of us—and not just from the outside. Through

---

14. Leon Cristiani, *Saint Margaret Mary Alacoque and the Promises of the Sacred Heart*, trans. M. Angeline Bouchard (Boston: St. Paul Editions, 1974), 82.

15. Cristiani, *Saint Margaret Mary*, 82–83.

his personal experience of taking on human nature, as well as the omniscience he possesses in his divine nature, Jesus knows and loves each of us from within. This divine love that God has in Christ for all people, which is made actual in his personal love for each and every human being, is key to understanding why Jesus chose to reveal his Sacred Heart to Margaret Mary for the benefit of the faithful.

During that initial revelation of the Sacred Heart, Margaret Mary experienced what she understood as Jesus granting her greater intimacy with him through a mystical union of her heart with his—and with it a greater share in the physical sufferings he underwent in his Passion. She received invisible stigmata, feeling as though her side was pierced with the lance that pierced Jesus after he died on the cross (John 19:34). And she perceived that Jesus, in granting her this pain, spoke words that effectively assured her that it was not a punishment but rather a sign of his close friendship with her: "And how have you been describing yourself up to the present: my slave? Well, now I'm giving you a new name: the beloved disciple of my Sacred Heart."[16] It was as though he was granting her, like St. John, a place beside him at table.

The second time that Jesus manifested his Sacred Heart to Margaret Mary is believed to have been on a first Friday in early 1674.

---

16. Alacoque, *Autobiography*, 45.

She received a vision of the wounded heart "in a throne of flames" and "transparent as crystal."[17] Encircling the heart were thorns, representing the sins of the faithful. Above it, a cross was suspended, "signifying that from the first instant of his Incarnation . . . the cross was implanted into it" as Jesus took on the sins of humanity that he would ultimately carry with him into his redemptive Passion.[18]

Margaret Mary wrote in her memoir that, in this vision, Jesus gave her to understand that he wished that "this Heart of God must be honored under the form of this heart of flesh."[19] He wanted the image of his Sacred Heart to be venerated by the faithful, and he wanted Margaret Mary personally to wear it over her own heart. In return, "he promised to pour out into the hearts of all those who honor the image of his Heart all the gifts it contains in fullness, and for all those who would wear this image on their persons [he promised] to imprint his love on their hearts and to destroy all unruly inclinations."[20]

The third revelation that Margaret Mary experienced of the Sacred Heart, which also took place in 1674, contained perhaps the most striking of all the images that she received. She saw Jesus

---

17. Cristiani, *Saint Margaret Mary*, 86.

18. Cristiani, *Saint Margaret Mary*, 86.

19. Cristiani, *Saint Margaret Mary*, 86.

20. Cristiani, *Saint Margaret Mary*, 86–87.

"in a blaze of glory—his five wounds shining like five suns."[21] Flames issued with special intensity from his chest, "which was like a furnace," and which he opened to reveal the source of the blaze—his Sacred Heart itself.[22]

Margaret Mary, recalling this encounter, said that Jesus explained to her that even greater than the pain he felt in his Passion was the pain he felt in receiving "ingratitude and indifference" from people in response to his redeeming love.[23] He asked her to compensate for such ingratitude to the best of her ability. When the nun protested that her own love could hardly make a difference, Jesus offered her divine assistance through the love of his own heart, which she experienced as a "scorching flame."[24] Not only was Jesus granting her—as he in some way grants each of us—the grace to return his love, but he was also demonstrating to her once again that his love is not perfunctory. It is personal and it is passionate. In effect, he was saying that if we cultivate devotion to him in his sacred humanity—a devotion that is accessible to us through contemplating his heart—we can gain the ability to love him as passionately as he loves us.

It was during this revelation that Margaret Mary heard Jesus instruct her to receive the Eucharist as often as her superior permitted her to do so, as well as on the first Friday of each month. In this way, the saint understood that Jesus was drawing a connection between devotion to his Sacred Heart and reception of

---

21. Alacoque, *Autobiography*, 46.

22. Alacoque, *Autobiography*, 46.

23. Alacoque, *Autobiography*, 46.

24. Alacoque, *Autobiography*, 46.

the Eucharist. This connection—which accords strongly with the witness of the Gospels, particularly John (see chapter one)—would become even more clear in Margaret Mary's fourth and final major revelation of the Sacred Heart.

Margaret Mary recounted in her memoir that she was kneeling before the Blessed Sacrament in June 1675, during the octave of Corpus Christi, when she experienced an overflow of graces from God. At that moment, she felt "inspired to make some return, and to give him love for love."[25] Once again Margaret Mary felt herself in the presence of Jesus as he showed her his heart, saying to her, "Behold this Heart, which has so loved people that it has spared nothing, even to the point of spending itself and being consumed to prove its love to them."[26] But instead of love, he said, he received only ingratitude: "Witness their irreverence, their sacrileges, their coldness and contempt for me in this sacrament of love."[27]

Then, Margaret Mary wrote, Jesus added, "What hurts me most is that hearts dedicated to my service"—that is, consecrated religious—"behave in this way." The nun then perceived from him words that would have a momentous impact upon the global church:

> That is why I am asking you to have the Friday after the octave of Corpus Christi set apart as a special feast in honor of my Heart—a day on which to receive me in holy

25. Alacoque, *Autobiography*, 77.

26. Cristiani, *Saint Margaret Mary*, 91.

27. Alacoque, *Autobiography*, 78.

Communion and make a solemn act of reparation for the indignities I have received in the Blessed Sacrament while exposed on the altars of the world.[28]

To this request for a Feast of the Sacred Heart, Margaret Mary recalled, Jesus added a promise. He would open his heart to all who gave him the honor that he desired and who brought others to do the same: "They will feel in all its fulness the power of my love."[29]

With those four revelations, we have the substance of St. Margaret Mary's experience of the Sacred Heart. Ten years would pass before her religious community, and the church at large, would learn of her revelations and begin to take them seriously. In the meantime, she confided her visions in the confessional to a young Jesuit priest, Father Claude La Colombière, SJ, who today is likewise a canonized saint.

Father Colombière, who had long fostered a devotion to the Heart of Jesus, was convinced of the veracity of Margaret Mary's visions and the other graces that she received.[30] During the time that he served as a visiting confessor at Paray, from February 1675

28. Alacoque, *Autobiography*, 78.

29. Alacoque, *Autobiography*, 78.

30. Unless otherwise noted, information on the life of St. Claude La Colombière, SJ, is taken from Georges Guitton, *Perfect Friend: The Life of Blessed Claude La Colombière, SJ, 1641–1682* (St. Louis: B. Herder, 1956).

to August 1676, he gave Margaret Mary great consolation as he affirmed that she was having authentic experiences of the presence of God. He also took seriously the request that she reported receiving from Jesus for the establishment of the feast of the Sacred Heart, particularly the call to reparation. However, he fell into ill health and died in 1682, when he was only forty-one. His greatest contribution to spreading devotion to the Sacred Heart came only after his death, and in a remarkable way.

One day in 1685, the nuns at Paray-le-Monial were dining together in the refectory. A designated lector read from the book that had been chosen for mealtime reading: *Spiritual Retreat*, a collection of Father Colombière's personal writings that was published after his death. Neither the lector nor any of the other nuns had vetted the book beforehand. They didn't have to, for he was known both at Paray and throughout France as an extraordinarily wise and holy priest.[31] The lector began to read a section where Colombière spoke of a devotion that God wished him to spread, which God himself had recommended to a person through revelations.

At that, the nuns' ears perked up. Only recently, their novice mistress, none other than Sister Margaret Mary, whom they knew had been among Colombière's directees, had suffered a reprimand from Mother Superior after she attempted to introduce devotion to the Sacred Heart into the novitiate. As the lector read on, the nuns heard Colombière's account of how he felt called to spread the devotion to the Sacred Heart that a woman he directed had received from the Lord. He included the description of the

---

31. In describing the reading of St. Claude La Colombière's book at a meal, I am relying on the account provided in Cristiani, *Saint Margaret Mary*, 113–114.

final revelation of the Sacred Heart as Margaret Mary had written it out for him, in her own words. Although Colombière did not mention Margaret Mary's name, all the nuns realized that the priest whom they so admired had faith in the truth of the devotion that she—without having told them of her revelations—had sought to promote. His endorsement of the Sacred Heart devotion led the Visitation nuns at Paray and beyond to promote it.

The devotion spread quickly, even more so after St. Margaret Mary's death in 1690, when her life and revelations were examined by theologians. Among the aspects of devotion to the Sacred Heart that the church examined and approved was a promise that Margaret Mary (in a letter to her mother superior, Mother de Saumaise) said she had received from Jesus:

> I promise you, in the excess of the mercy of my Heart, that my almighty love will grant to all those who take communion on the nine first Fridays of the month in succession, the grace of final perseverance. They will not die in my displeasure, nor without receiving the sacraments, if necessary, and my divine Heart will be a safe asylum for them in that final hour.[32]

Father Ottavio De Bertolis, SJ, vice rector of the Church of the Gesù in Rome, observes that, although receiving Holy Communion every First Friday for nine months straight may not seem difficult to us, seventeenth-century Catholics would have perceived it much differently. At that time, "people no longer

---

32. Ottavio De Bertolis, "350 Years Since the Apparitions at Paray-le-Monial," March 6, 2024, *La Civiltà Cattolica*, https://www.laciviltacattolica.com/350-years-since-the-apparitions-at-paray-le-monial/.

approached the sacraments as frequently as today, since so much emphasis was placed on the seriousness of sin, the need for proper penance, and the inner dispositions required to receive Communion worthily."[33]

Jesus's promise, then, is really an invitation to be unafraid to receive him in the Eucharist. What is more, it is a self-fulfilling promise in the sense that the grace of final perseverance comes naturally to people who have formed their spiritual life around the rhythms of the church's liturgical calendar and regular reception of the sacraments. In that light, De Bertolis writes, the commitment to observe the First Friday devotion is "easily transformed into [seeking] more frequent access to the sacrament of penance and will tend to extend into lengthier times of adoration, and thus into a deeper union with the Lord, which will certainly manifest its fruits in a more intense and fervent Christian life."[34] And so, in addition to the literal meaning of Jesus's promise, we can also find a symbolic one: "those 'nine' Fridays may indeed recall the nine months of gestation, as if the soul is somehow regenerated by the Spirit, as it was for nine months in the womb."[35] The end result is new life in the love of the heart of Christ.

There is yet much in St. Margaret Mary's revelations for us to unpack. In chapter five, we will see how Pius XII, in his encyclical on the Sacred Heart, gave the church a helpful key to interpreting them. But first, we will look at the spiritual life of a nun closer to our own time who, like Margaret Mary, conveyed a message of divine love to a world in desperate need of it.

---

33. De Bertolis, "350 Years."

34. De Bertolis, "350 Years."

35. De Bertolis, "350 Years."

Chapter Four

The Heart of Mercy
St. Faustina Kowalska

⸻

Although St. Faustina Kowalska (1905–1938) lived more than two hundred years after St. Margaret Mary, the visions of the Heart of Jesus that she reported, like those of her seventeenth-century predecessor, had special relevance for the faithful of her era. During St. Margaret Mary's time, besides the heresy of Jansenism, which led Catholics to be afraid of approaching Jesus in the Eucharist,[1] Catholic faith also faced the challenge of rationalism, which claimed that the human mind was the only source of truth. The revelations granted to Margaret Mary were a powerful counter to rationalism because through them, a modern author notes, "we were brought back to the 'heart,' and not the 'mind,' to the symbol, and not the definition."[2]

---

1. On Jansenist spirituality, see James Hitchcock, *History of the Catholic Church* (San Francisco: Ignatius Press, 2012), 313.

2. De Bertolis, "350 Years."

By the time Faustina began to receive her revelations in a Polish convent during the early 1930s, the Jansenist heresy had faded. Rationalism remained, now in the guise of Marxism. But the most pressing challenge to faith was not from any single ideology. Rather, it was the pessimism that had overtaken young adults in the wake of what was then called the Great War and is now known as World War I.

Highly touted thinkers such as H.G. Wells assured the Allied Powers that, by engaging the Central Powers, they would fight "the war to end all wars." Instead, not only did the war result in some twenty million deaths, twenty-one million injuries, and untold emotional trauma, it also exacerbated political and economic tensions that would in time erupt into World War II. The generation that came of age during World War I came to be known as the Lost Generation. Lacking the confidence in the future that helped their parents overcome difficult times, these people struggled to find a sense of purpose.

It was a time when people around the world, having undergone extreme forms of suffering—and unknowingly about to face the horrors of World War II—were in desperate need of knowing that God was with them in the midst of their suffering, confusion, and despair. The words that Faustina reported hearing from Jesus met that need by offering a divine olive branch to the war-torn human race: "I do not want to punish aching mankind, but I desire to heal it, pressing it to My Merciful Heart. I use punishment when they themselves force Me to do so; My hand is reluctant to take hold of the sword of justice. Before the Day of Justice I am sending the Day of Mercy."[3]

The young nun who would become known as St. Faustina was baptized Helena Kowalska two days after her birth in 1905. The third of ten children, she was born into a Catholic family of modest means in Głogowiec, a village in central Poland.[4]

There are certain similarities in Faustina Kowalska's early history to that of St. Margaret Mary. She felt called to the religious life very early, when she was just seven years old. After she reached her teens, when she asserted her desire to enter the convent, her family refused to give their permission. However, Faustina resolved the tensions with her family at a younger age than did Margaret Mary. At eighteen, following a revelation from Jesus where she heard him urge her to stop putting him off, she gained the courage to walk out of the family home with nothing but the dress on her back.

---

3. Faustina Kowalska, *Divine Mercy in My Soul: The Diary of St. Maria Faustina Kowalska*, 3rd ed. (Stockbridge, MA: Marian Press, 2008), §1588. In the introduction to this edition of Faustina's diary, M. Elizabeth Siepak lists no fewer than six key manifestations of the Divine Mercy devotion, including the Divine Mercy Chaplet and the Hour of Mercy. Here I wish to focus upon the central aspect of the devotion—namely, the image and how it can serve to inflame and deepen our devotion to the Heart of Jesus.

4. Unless otherwise noted, all biographical details of St. Faustina's life are drawn from Faustina Kowalska, *Divine Mercy in My Soul*.

Faustina traveled to Warsaw, where she felt called to enter the Congregation of the Sisters of Our Lady of Mercy. But the superior, who judged her to be "no one special," declined to accept her unless she could provide the funds to pay for her clothing. Undeterred, Faustina found work as a domestic servant for a pious Catholic woman. It took her a full year to save enough money so that she could reapply at the convent, but once she did, in August 1925, she was accepted. Eight months later, after completing her postulancy, she received the habit and her name in religion: Sister Maria Faustina of the Blessed Sacrament.

During the eleven years when her health permitted her to do active work in the convent, Faustina was sent to different houses of her religious congregation according to its needs. Since she had received only three years of formal education as a child, all the jobs she was given were menial; she worked as a cook, a gardener, and a gatekeeper. But although on the outside there was little to distinguish her from other humble nuns, Faustina had an extraordinarily deep interior life, living in union with Jesus and in what she perceived as a frequent (perhaps even near-constant) dialogue with him.

What we know of Faustina's interior life comes from a series of notebooks she kept, beginning in 1934, that are collectively known as her diary. In it, she described visions and locutions she had received, and provided spiritual interpretations of events in her life. Faustina admitted frankly in her diary that in her early years as a nun, she was frightened and discouraged at the thought of suffering, knowing herself to be weak and incapable of handling it on her own. "So," she wrote, "I prayed continuously, asking Jesus to strengthen me and to grant me the power of his

Holy Spirit that I might carry out His holy will in all things."
She drew comfort by contrasting her own smallness with God's
greatness, and her own deficiencies with God's abundance: "In
my own interior life, I am looking with one eye at the abyss of
my misery and baseness, and with the other, at the abyss of Your
mercy, O God."[5]

On the evening of February 22, 1931, the first Sunday of Lent,
Faustina received a dramatic vision in which Jesus gave her a new
mission. She had returned to her cell after praying Vespers with
her community when, she wrote, Jesus appeared to her wearing a
white garment. "One hand [was] raised in the gesture of blessing,
the other was touching the garment at the breast. From beneath
the garment, slightly drawn aside at the breast, there were ema-
nating two large rays, one red, the other pale."[6] Awestruck, yet
joyful, Faustina gazed for some time in silent adoration. Then
she heard Jesus say, "Paint an image according to the pattern you
see, with the signature: 'Jesus, I trust in You.' I desire that this
image be venerated, first in your chapel, and [then] throughout
the world."

Faustina wrote that Jesus then attached several promises to
the image, saying, "I promise that the soul that will venerate this

5. Kowalska, *Divine Mercy*, §55.

6. Kowalska, *Divine Mercy*, §47.

image will not perish. I also promise victory over [its] enemies already here on earth, especially at the hour of death. I Myself will defend it as My own glory."[7]

At the time that she received the revelation of the Divine Mercy image, Faustina did not yet understand the symbolic meaning of the two rays that emanated from Jesus's chest. Three years later, when her confessor instructed her to ask Jesus what the rays meant, she prayed for guidance and heard the words: "The two rays denote Blood and Water. The pale ray stands for the Water which makes souls righteous. The red ray stands for the Blood which is the life of souls. These two rays issued forth from the very depths of My tender mercy when My agonized Heart was opened by a lance on the Cross."[8] In other words, Faustina perceived that Jesus intended the rays to represent the mystical meaning of his side wound as the church has understood it from its earliest centuries—as the source of the sacraments, particularly the two main sacraments of the Eucharist (represented by blood) and Baptism (represented by water).[9]

The nun knew that she could not act on such a revelation without first submitting it to the judgment of the church. She went to her confessor to report what she had seen and heard. But the priest was not ready to believe that Jesus, even if he were

---

7. Kowalska, *Divine Mercy*, §47.

8. Kowalska, *Divine Mercy*, §299.

9. See the discussion of John 19:34 in chapter one.

appearing to Faustina, really intended that she have a devotional painting made. "That [vision] refers to your soul," the confessor told Faustina. "Certainly, paint God's image in your soul."[10]

In her diary, Faustina recounted that after she emerged from the confessional, she heard Jesus say, "My image already is in your soul." He then expanded upon his wishes for the mission that he had given her: "I desire that there be a Feast of Mercy. I want this image, which you will paint with a brush, to be solemnly blessed on the first Sunday after Easter; that Sunday is to be the Feast of Mercy."[11]

Faustina wrote that she then heard Jesus explain what he intended to achieve through what would come to be known as the Divine Mercy image: "I desire that priests proclaim this great mercy of mine toward souls of sinners. Let the sinner not be afraid to approach me. The flames of mercy are burning me—clamoring to be spent; I want to pour them out upon these souls."[12]

In years to come, when the church judged Faustina's visions, the theologians who cleared them for approval found in them the same voice of Jesus who, in the Gospel reading for the Solemnity of the Sacred Heart, cries out: "Come to me, all you who labor

---

10. Kowalska, *Divine Mercy*, §49.

11. Kowalska, *Divine Mercy*, §49.

12. Kowalska, *Divine Mercy*, §50.

and are burdened, and I will give you rest. Take my yoke upon you and learn from me, for I am meek and humble of heart; and you will find rest for yourselves. For my yoke is easy, and my burden light" (Matthew 11:28–30). The Divine Mercy message Faustina received, at its core, distills the revelation of the Sacred Heart to its most basic element: Jesus's great love that simultaneously calls sinners (meaning every human being who has ever lived, except his mother)[13] to turn to him and offers them the grace to do so.

However, for Faustina to spread the message of Divine Mercy, she first had to fulfill what she perceived as Jesus's command to have the image painted. In trying to accomplish her task, she faced seemingly insurmountable obstacles. She lacked the skill to paint the image herself, neither could she afford to commission a painting. Finally, frustrated and exhausted, she approached Father Jósef Andrasz, SJ, who was then serving as a visiting confessor at her congregation's novitiate. In the confessional, Faustina explained her situation and asked the Jesuit to dispense her from having to obey her perceived revelations.

Father Andrasz was the editor of the *Messenger of the Sacred Heart*, the Polish newsletter for the Apostleship of Prayer—the Jesuit-run fellowship dedicated to spreading devotion to the Heart of Jesus. He readily recognized the spiritual value of

---

13. The Blessed Virgin Mary's freedom from sin is itself a gift from the Heart of Jesus. Because he, in his divine nature, is outside of time, Jesus was able to redeem Mary through the foreseen merits that he would win for the human race on the cross. In the words of Pope Pius IX, "The most Blessed Virgin Mary was, from the first moment of her conception, by a singular grace and privilege of almighty God and by virtue of the merits of Jesus Christ, Savior of the human race, preserved immune from all stain of original sin" (*Catechism*, §491).

Faustina's reported revelations. Once the nun finished speaking, he gave her his answer—but it was not what she expected. "I will dispense you from nothing, Sister," Andrasz said. "It is not right for you to turn away from these interior inspirations, but you must absolutely—and I say, absolutely—speak about them to your [regular] confessor; otherwise you will go astray despite the great graces you are receiving from God."[14] The Jesuit added that it was imperative that Faustina find a permanent confessor to serve as her spiritual director.[15]

Andrasz's reply greatly upset Faustina. "I thought that I would get myself free from everything," she wrote, "and it turned out quite the opposite—an explicit command to follow the requests of Jesus."[16] Plus she had to find a spiritual director whom she would feel comfortable telling about her revelations, which seemed almost as impossible as finding a painter.

Utterly perplexed, Faustina prayed for mercy. Soon after, her prayers were answered, as she was sent to her congregation's convent in Vilnius, where she met Father Michał Sopoćko, whom she recognized as the man whom God had designated to be her spiritual director. Sopoćko, whom the church today calls Blessed (the final level of recognition before canonization), not only gave Faustina the guidance she needed but also accepted from her the responsibility of promoting the Divine Mercy devotion, which he considered a true message from God.

---

14. Kowalska, *Divine Mercy*, §52.

15. Kowalska, *Divine Mercy*, §52.

16. Kowalska, *Divine Mercy*, §53.

Within months of meeting St. Faustina, Father Sopoćko had found an accomplished local artist, Eugeniusz Kazimirowski, to paint the Divine Mercy image under Faustina's direction. However, when she went with her Mother Superior to see the completed, or near-completed, image at the artist's studio in June 1934, she was crushed to discover that his depiction of Jesus was nowhere near as beautiful as the Lord appeared in her visions.

Faustina wrote in her diary that upon returning to her convent from Kazimirowski's studio, she "went immediately to the chapel and wept a good deal."[17] She said to Jesus, "Who will paint you as beautiful as you are?"[18] And in reply, she heard the words, "Not in the beauty of the color, nor of the brush lies the greatness of this image, but in my grace."[19]

An important aspect of the image's greatness lies in the inscription that appears at the bottom. As the image was being completed, Father Sopoćko checked with Faustina to confirm what the inscription was to say and where it was to be placed in the painting. The nun prayed and perceived that Jesus answered her, "I am offering people a vessel with which they are to keep coming for graces to the fountain of mercy. That vessel is this image with the signature: 'Jesus, I trust in you.'"[20]

---

17. Kowalska, *Divine Mercy*, §313.

18. Kowalska, *Divine Mercy*, §313.

19. Kowalska, *Divine Mercy*, §313.

20. Kowalska, *Divine Mercy*, §327.

How exactly does "Jesus, I trust in you" fit with the Divine Mercy message? Many years later, Pope St. John Paul II, in his homily at St. Faustina's canonization in 2000, described the prayer as a "simple act of abandonment to Jesus [that] dispels the thickest clouds and lets a ray of light penetrate every life."[21]

Faustina's diary contains a practical example of what such trustful abandonment looks like when practiced in daily life: an exchange that the saint described having with Jesus on October 10, 1937, as her health was declining due to tuberculosis.

"Through the vows [of religious life]," Faustina prayed, "I have given myself entirely to you; I have then nothing more that I can offer you."[22]

The saint then heard Jesus say, "My daughter, you have not offered me that which is really yours." Faustina examined her mind and heart but could not find anything she had not yet offered the Lord. "Jesus," she said, "tell me what it is, and I will give it to you at once with a generous heart." She perceived the voice of Jesus respond with kindness: "Daughter, give Me your misery, because it is your exclusive property." At that moment, Faustina wrote:

> A ray of light illumined my soul, and I saw the whole abyss of my misery. In that same moment I nestled close to the Most Sacred Heart of Jesus with so much trust that even if I had the sins of all the damned weighing on my conscience,

21. John Paul II, "Mass in St. Peter's Square for the Canonization of Sr. Mary Faustina Kowalska," homily, St. Peter's Square, Vatican City," April 30, 2000, https://www.vatican.va/content/john-paul-ii/en/homilies/2000/documents/hf_jp-ii_hom_20000430_faustina.html.

22. Kowalska, *Divine Mercy*, §1318.

> I would not have doubted God's mercy but, with a heart crushed to dust, I would have thrown myself into the abyss of Your mercy. I believe, O Jesus, that you would not reject me, but would absolve me through the hand of your representative.

These reflections of Faustina, written less than a year before her death on October 5, 1938, reveal that, for her, the Divine Mercy message was about "[nestling] close to the Most Sacred Heart of Jesus." Pope John Paul, in his homily at her canonization, established Divine Mercy Sunday (the feast that Faustina reported Jesus wished to be celebrated on the First Sunday after Easter), and he echoed her words: "Divine Mercy reaches human beings through the heart of Christ crucified. . . . It is not a new message but can be considered a gift of special enlightenment that helps us to relive the Gospel of Easter more intensely, to offer it as a ray of light to the men and women of our time."[23]

For those who had long supported the Divine Mercy message, John Paul's praise of Faustina's revelations came as a vindication, for the message was mired for many years in a controversy that seems bizarre today. The dispute began in 1958, when an Italian translation of Faustina's diary came to the attention of Vatican officials. Unfortunately, the translation contained numerous errors, some of which amounted to outright heresies.

In 1959, the Holy See's doctrinal office (which apparently did not have any Polish readers on staff) issued a notification that barred Catholics from spreading the Divine Mercy devotion until concerns about Faustina's diary could be clarified. Over

---

23. John Paul II, "Canonization of Sr. Mary Faustina Kowalska."

the next several years, several Polish bishops, including Kraków Archbishop Karol Wojtyła (the future John Paul II) urged Vatican officials to speed up their study of the diary, which they knew to be perfectly orthodox. However, time moves differently at the Holy See. Nearly twenty years passed before the Sacred Congregation for the Canonization of Saints finally lifted the ban, having determined that Faustina's diary contained nothing against the Catholic faith.[24]

When Faustina's account of her private revelations finally became accessible again, Catholic readers found them to be in deep harmony with the teachings on the Sacred Heart that were promulgated by Pope Pius XII after Faustina's death. So we will now delve into Pius's teachings, which in turn greatly inspired holy people whose lives we will explore in subsequent chapters, namely, Catherine and Eddie Doherty, and Father Pedro Arrupe, SJ.

---

24. For the history of the Vatican's ban of the Divine Mercy devotion, see Michael Gaitley, *The Second Greatest Story Ever Told* (Marian Press: Stockbridge, MA, 2015), 65–69.

Chapter Five

The Heart
of the Church

Pope Pius XII

─────────◆─────────

After traversing the heights of the private revelations of St. Margaret Mary and St. Faustina, the idea of exploring the writings of Pope Pius XII (1876–1958)—or any pope—may feel like a jarring fall back down to earth. This is a book of spirituality, after all. Why bother to delve into dull doctrine that can easily be found in the *Catechism* when the church's history offers us tales of saints whose visions provide ample inspiration for our personal devotion?

The short answer is that the saints, past and present, were women and men who thought with the church. They listened to what the church taught and sought to frame their own prayer lives around those teachings. When they received private revelations, they submitted them to the judgment of the church's representatives.

It might be objected that visionaries such as Margaret Mary and Faustina, who had very little in the way of formal religious education, lived much (perhaps all) of their lives without reading any papal encyclicals. And that's true! But they sought out the guidance of learned spiritual directors—priests who had studied official Catholic teaching—and through such guidance they came to understand more fully the visions they had received. If we wish "to comprehend with all the holy ones what is the breadth and length and height and depth, and to know the love of Christ that surpasses knowledge" so that we "may be filled with all the fullness of God" (Ephesians 3:18–19), we would do well to drink from that same wellspring.

But the main reason I want to share the spirituality of the Sacred Heart as it was taught by Pius XII is because, ever since I first discovered it as a new convert to Catholicism, I have been in love with it. And I'm not alone. When the world's bishops came together in the early 1960s for the Second Vatican Council, the documents that they produced cited Pius XII's writings more often than any other authority, apart from the Bible. Pius XII's spirituality has become part of how the church understands itself and its relationship to Christ—and it is deeply rooted in devotion to the Heart of Jesus.

The starting point of Pius's spirituality is the love that Jesus bears for every individual human being. When Pius discusses Jesus's love for individuals, he extends it to its natural consequence, namely, that the church should always keep the good of each person within sight, even as it ministers to the masses. In the words of theologian Anna Rowlands, "As Christians we are called to follow Christ in seeing the multitude and having pity upon them; however, Pius emphasizes that truly seeing the multitude requires a capacity to see and hear the unique, unrepeatable person."[1]

Pius employs that same dual lens—viewing the whole of humanity through its individual members—in his writings that bring to light his spirituality of the Heart of Jesus. Although his most important writing on the topic is his 1956 encyclical letter on devotion to the Sacred Heart, *Haurietis aquas*, the teachings he put forth in that document build upon ones he had developed more than ten years earlier in the 1943 encyclical *Mystici corporis Christi* (*On the Mystical Body of Christ*). For that reason, before looking directly at his teachings on the Sacred Heart, it's worth taking a moment to discover the profound insights of *Mystici corporis*, especially given its importance for Vatican II and for Catholic life and worship today.

In *Mystici corporis*, Pius seeks to express what the church is. Too often, when we think about the church, we think about the hierarchy as separate from the laity—and sometimes we commit the opposite error by thinking of the laity as separate from the hierarchy. For Pius, the church is all of its people—and much more. He defines it simply as the Mystical Body of Christ.

To untrained ears, "mystical body" can sound spooky, but that's not how Pius intends the term. He uses the adjective *mystical* as a counterpart to *real*. Jesus has a real body that walked the

---

1. Anna Rowlands, *Towards a Politics of Communion: Catholic Social Teaching in Dark Times* (London: Bloomsbury, 2021), 49.

earth and is now, in its resurrected state, alive in heaven. His real body is what we receive in the Eucharist at every Mass. At the same time, Jesus also has a Mystical Body that extends his presence on earth through time. His Mystical Body also extends his presence into purgatory, and it extends his presence to fill heaven. It is the Catholic Church and every individual in it.

Here is where Pius's spirituality becomes intriguing. On the one hand, he directly identifies the Mystical Body of Christ with the Catholic Church. He grounds this identification in sacred Scripture, particularly St. Paul's words in his letter to the Colossians: "Now I rejoice in my sufferings for your sake, and in my flesh I am filling up what is lacking in the afflictions of Christ on behalf of his body, which is the church."[2] On the other hand, he insists that, if we have "true love" of the Mystical Body, "we should recognize in other men and women, although they are not yet joined to us in the body of the Church, our brothers and sisters in Christ according to the flesh, called, together with us, to the same eternal salvation."[3]

Pius's teaching on non-Catholics sharing Catholics' call to salvation was remarkable for its time. When he was writing in 1943, nearly twenty years before Vatican II, the Catholic Church was still a long way away from having official relations with non-Catholic religions, let alone with nonreligious people. Only

---

2. Pius XII, Encyclical Letter *Mystici corporis Christi* (*On the Mystical Body of Christ*), June 29, 1943, §1 https://www.vatican.va/content/pius-xii/en/encyclicals/documents/hf_p-xii_enc_29061943_mystici-corporis-christi.html. Authors writing about the encyclical usually call it by the abbreviated title *Mystici corporis*, so I have done so here.

3. Pius XII, *Mystici corporis*, §26, quoting Colossians 1:24.

with the Council would the church come to not only sanction but even encourage Catholics to engage in dialogue with their non-Catholic neighbors. But Pius felt strongly that if the members of the Mystical Body were to practice the love of neighbor that the Gospels commanded, they needed to recognize Christ even in those who were "not yet joined" to him by baptism, and might never be.[4]

Thirteen years later, with *Haurietis aquas* (*On Devotion to the Sacred Heart*), Pius built upon the connections he drew in *Mystici corporis* between love of God, love of neighbor, and the union to which all humanity is called in Christ—emphasizing that, for the Christian, these three things are inseparable. Because Jesus, through the love of his Sacred Heart, seeks to draw all of humanity to himself, all who are united with him through baptism are called to engage in "contemplation of, and a devotion to, the mystery of God's merciful love for the human race."[5]

The title of *Haurietis aquas* comes from the encyclical's first line, a verse from the prophet Isaiah (Isaiah 12:3) that Pius quotes from the Vulgate (St. Jerome's Latin translation of the Bible): "You shall

---

4. Although I don't intend to enter into the so-called "Pius War" here (that is, the discussion of whether or not Pius XII did enough to protest the Holocaust), it is worth noting that *Mystici corporis* goes on to denounce those who practice racial hatred (see *Mystici corporis*, §96). Readers of the time understood that the targets of Pius's denunciation included Nazi Germany.

5. Pius XII, *Haurietis aquas*, §97.

draw waters with joy out of the Savior's fountain."[6] Pius, drawing upon the tradition of the church, finds the fulfillment of Isaiah's image in Jesus, whom St. John's Gospel identifies as the source of "living waters" that are the only thing truly capable of satisfying the thirst of the human race (see John 4:10 and 7:37–38).

For the present-day reader, it is interesting to see how concerned Pius is to answer critics of devotion to the Sacred Heart. Those who look to the 1950s as a golden age of Catholic piety might be surprised to discover that many of the same objections to devotion to the Heart of Jesus that people have today were also made back then—and they were made loudly enough to be heard in Rome.

Pius laments that there are some who, "led astray by prejudices, sometimes go so far as to consider this devotion ill-adapted, not to say detrimental, to the more pressing spiritual needs of the Church and humanity in this present age."[7] He likewise expresses distress that some confuse the devotion's nature with "various individual forms of piety which the church approves and encourages but does not command" or see it as "a kind of additional practice which each one may take up or not according to his own inclination."[8]

The pope also criticizes those who object to devotion to the Sacred Heart of Jesus on the grounds of machismo. He divides these into two groups (though I don't think he intends to imply that they are mutually exclusive). First, Pius writes against those who think that the Sacred Heart is useless to "men who are fighting in the army of the divine King."[9] He has in mind what we would

---

6. Pius XII, *Haurietis aquas*, §1, quoting Isaiah 12:3.

7. Pius XII, *Haurietis aquas*, §10.

8. Pius XII, *Haurietis aquas*, §10.

9. Pius XII, *Haurietis aquas*, §11.

call today the culture-warrior mindset (a way of thinking that, it should be noted, is not limited to men). Such people "are inspired mainly by the thought of laboring with their own strength, their own resources and expenditures of their own time, to defend Catholic truth, to teach and spread it, to instill Christian social teachings, to promote those acts of religion and those undertakings which they consider much more necessary today."[10]

The other macho group that Pius criticizes comprises those who object to a devotion that they perceive as insufficiently intellectual or spiritual. Such people assume that devotion to the Sacred Heart is based on feelings and is "consequently more suited to the use of women, since it seems to them something not quite suitable for educated men."[11]

Although Pius will go on to condemn that objection, along with all the others, for being "in entire disagreement" with the teachings of the Church,[12] he doesn't elaborate on why it is so offensive to deride devotion to the Sacred Heart as being for women only. It helps to know that Pius was ahead of his time in advocating for women's rights, advocating as far back as 1947 for "equality of salary, for men and women, provided there be equal work and output."[13] He had little patience for men who belittled women's capabilities or spiritual practices.

10. Pius XII, *Haurietis aquas*, §11.

11. Pius XII, *Haurietis aquas*, §12.

12. Pius XII, *Haurietis aquas*, §14.

13. Pius XII, "Papal Directives for the Woman of Today," speech, Congress of the International Union of Catholic Women's League, September 11, 1947, Rome, *EWTN*, https://www.ewtn.com/catholicism/library/papal-directives-for-the-woman-of-today-8962.

One last objection that Pius notes is made by those who "consider a devotion of this kind as primarily demanding penance, expiation and the other virtues which they call 'passive,' meaning thereby that they produce no external results."[14] It is the same attitude that Pope John Paul II would later deride as a "cult of action."[15] Pius characterizes it as the mistaken belief that "to re-enkindle the spirit of piety in modern times," Catholics "should aim at open and vigorous action, at the triumph of the Catholic faith, at a strong defense of Christian morals."[16]

If it is difficult to understand what Pius means when he criticizes the cult of action as being in opposition to devotion to the Heart of Jesus, it might help to think of it as a "cult of success." In its idolatry of external results, it discounts the value of personal conversion, which is an essentially interior process. Cardinal Joseph Ratzinger, the future Pope Benedict XVI, was concerned about that same mindset when he told an assembly of catechists to beware "the temptation of impatience, the temptation of immediately finding the great success, in finding large numbers." Ratzinger then cited a favorite proverb of his: "Success is not one of the names of God."[17]

14. Pius XII, *Haurietis aquas*, §13.

15. John Paul II, *Reconciliatio et paenitentia*, §18.

16. Pius XII, *Haurietis aquas*, §13.

17. Joseph Ratzinger, "The New Evangelization: Building the Civilization of Love," December 10, 2000, Servants of the Pierced Hearts of Jesus and Mary (website), https://www.piercedhearts.org/benedict_xvi/Cardinal%20Ratzinger/new_evangelization.htm.

After criticizing the critics, Pius in *Haurietis aquas* moved on to his main objective in writing the encyclical: to teach that, for the Christian believer, devotion to the Heart of Jesus was not only healthy but even necessary for growth in the spiritual life. To understand his intentions, it will help to have some knowledge of the state of the church's theology of the Sacred Heart at the time of his writing.

During the eighteenth and nineteenth centuries, as Catholic theologians examined the revelations given to St. Margaret Mary, they came to identify two key aspects of the spirituality of the Sacred Heart, which they called by the Latin terms *redamatio* and *reparatio*.[18] *Redamatio* means "returning love" and *reparatio* means "making reparation." *Redamatio* is the first movement that our heart experiences when we encounter the love of Jesus's Heart: Jesus inflames our heart with his love and makes us want to give love back to him. Then, as we return Jesus's love, our heart feels further moved to engage in *reparatio*, for we feel that it is not enough simply to love him back. We want to do something more: to make up for the times when we have failed to love him or our neighbor as we should and to make up for others' failings.

At the time that Pius XII set out to write *Haurietis aquas*, he did so with the awareness that the previous papal encyclical devoted to the Sacred Heart, his predecessor Pius XI's *Miserentissimus Redemptor*, was almost entirely concerned with *reparatio*. Its very subtitle was "On Reparation to the Sacred

---

18. I am indebted to Gregory Gresko's research for my understanding of the concepts of *redamatio* and *reparatio*. See Gregory Gresko, "The Consecration of the Family to the Heart of Jesus and the Pastoral Approach of Father Mateo Crawley-Boevey, SS.CC" (Rome: SThD diss., Pontifical John Paul II Institute for Studies on Marriage and Family, 2014).

Heart"; the word "reparation" appeared in the encyclical's English-language translation twelve times. But in the English-language translation of *Haurietis aquas*, which is about five times as long as *Miserentissimus Redemptor*, the word "reparation" appears only three times. It seems that Pius XII felt that a course correction was in order.

Much like Pope Francis, who, while acknowledging the reality of sin, felt the need to counter a trend toward rigorism by consistently reminding the faithful of God's mercy, Pius XII felt that talk of *reparatio* needed to be counterbalanced with talk of *redamatio*. And his attitude makes sense. The degree to which we are moved to make reparation to the Sacred Heart depends upon the degree to which we are moved to return Jesus's love. So Pius used *Haurietis aquas* as an opportunity to return to a discussion of first principles: how God loves us and how we are to love God.

Pius notes in the encyclical that, whereas prior to the Incarnation God loved humanity only with a spiritual love, "the love which breathes from the Gospel, from the letters of the Apostles and the pages of the Apocalypse—all of which portray the love of the Heart of Jesus Christ—expresses not only divine love but also human sentiments of love."[19] Although the Psalms, Song of Songs, and the prophets all likened God's love to human love, only with Jesus's birth could God *actually* love humanity with human love.

The Incarnation therefore makes a real difference in how we, as human beings, become capable of understanding God's love for us. Pius is emphatic on that point because he wants the

---

19. Pius XII, *Haurietis aquas*, §38.

reader to understand why devotion to Jesus's Sacred Heart is not optional for Catholics. It is in fact necessary for our spiritual maturity and growth because it compels us to confront the reality of Jesus's humanity and thus the redemption he won for us upon the cross.

To what exactly are we applying our minds and hearts when we are devoted to the Sacred Heart? Pius answers that "the Heart of the Incarnate Word is deservedly and rightly considered the chief sign and symbol of that threefold love with which the divine Redeemer unceasingly loves His eternal Father and all mankind."[20] By "threefold love," Pius means:

1. "that divine love which [Jesus] shares with the Father and the Holy Spirit but which He, the Word made flesh, alone manifests through a weak and perishable body, since 'in Him dwells the fullness of the Godhead bodily'";[21]
2. "that burning love which, infused into His soul, enriches the human will of Christ and enlightens and governs its acts by the most perfect knowledge";[22] and

20. Pius XII, *Haurietis aquas*, §54.

21. Pius XII, *Haurietis aquas*, §55, quoting Colossians 2:9.

22. Pius XII, *Haurietis aquas*, §56. The church uses the verb *infused* when describing how Jesus receives knowledge directly from God through the union of his divine nature with his human nature.

3. "sensible love," meaning the love that is felt and expressed through the senses, "since the body of Jesus Christ, formed by the Holy Spirit, in the womb of the Virgin Mary, possesses full powers of feelings and perception, in fact, more so than any other human body."[23]

The Heart of Jesus, in symbolizing this threefold love, is not only a fitting object of our devotion but also, Pius writes, "a sort of mystical ladder by which we mount to the embrace of 'God our Savior.'"[24] We are therefore not to think of it as having "suddenly appeared in the Church" due to a private revelation. "Rather," Pius says, "it has blossomed forth of its own accord as a result of that lively faith and burning devotion of men and women who were endowed with heavenly gifts, and who were drawn toward the adorable Redeemer and His glorious wounds which they saw as irresistible proofs of that unbounded love."[25] In other words, Pius says:

> It is clear that the revelations made to St. Margaret Mary brought nothing new into Catholic doctrine. Their importance lay in this that Christ Our Lord, exposing His Sacred Heart, wished in a quite extraordinary way to invite the minds of men to a contemplation of, and a devotion to, the mystery of God's merciful love for the human race.[26]

---

23. Pius XII, *Haurietis aquas*, §57.

24. Pius XII, *Haurietis aquas*, §58, quoting Titus 3:4.

25. Pius XII, *Haurietis aquas*, §96. The word "adorable" here stands in for the Latin term *adorandi*, which literally means "worthy of adoration."

26. Pius XII, *Haurietis aquas*, §97.

Like a good teacher, having spoken of the great importance that devotion to the Sacred Heart has for the Christian life, Pius then adds a necessary distinction. (His style reminds me of a seminary rector I knew who, after making a dramatic point in his Sunday homilies, would add, "Now, don't hear what I'm not saying.") Pius says that, because the devotion in question is by its very nature heart-to-Heart, the faithful accomplish it primarily through interior acts of piety—not by placing themselves in pews on First Fridays. Likewise, he adds, the essence of devotion to the Sacred Heart is not found in obtaining the benefits that St. Margaret Mary reported were promised by Jesus to those who practiced it. "For," Pius writes, "if Christ has solemnly promised [such benefits] in private revelations, it was for the purpose of encouraging men and women to perform with greater fervor the chief duties of the Catholic religion, namely, love and expiation, and thus take all possible measures for their own spiritual advantage."[27]

So devotion to the Sacred Heart really is all about love—a love that, Pius observes, is desperately needed, given that we see "so many evils . . . [that] cause sharp conflict among individuals, families, nations and the whole world, particularly today more than at any other time."[28]

Pius's words are a somber reminder that the era following World War II, which some point to as a golden age because of the numerical strength of the Catholic Church in Europe and the United States, did not seem so golden to those who were in

---

27. Pius XII, *Haurietis aquas*, §112.

28. Pius XII, *Haurietis aquas*, §120.

the midst of it. Then as now, people worried greatly about tensions both near and far. But, as Pius adds, thankfully "the love of Christ—which devotion to the Sacred Heart of Jesus daily increases and fosters more and more—can move the faithful to bring into the activities of life the Law of the Gospel." In any case, he says, it is only by living the gospel that we can attain "peace [that is] worthy of the name."[29]

We need that peace today every bit as much as people needed it in 1956. Jesus shows us the way, for he is the way.[30]

---

29. Pius XII, *Haurietis aquas*, §120.

30. See John 14:6, which Pius quotes in *Haurietis aquas*, §14.

Chapter Six

The Heart of Service

Julia Greeley

———◆———

Julia Greeley was a woman of extraordinary charity who died in Denver, Colorado, in 1918. She is not yet an officially recognized saint of the Catholic Church; currently, she bears the title Servant of God, which is given to those in the earliest stage of the canonization process. But, having read about her life, I think of her as a saint of a special kind: an invisible saint.[1] In calling Julia invisible, I don't merely mean that that she chose to do her

---

1. All biographical information about Julia Greeley in this chapter is taken from Blaine Burkey, ed., *In Secret Service of the Sacred Heart: Remembering the Life and Virtues of Denver's Angel of Charity, the Servant of God Julia Greeley, O.F.S.* (Denver: Julia Greeley Guild, 2019), PDF, the updated edition of a work originally published in 2012. Published by the guild that is promoting Julia's cause for canonization, *In Secret Service of the Sacred Heart* is the most comprehensive source available on Julia's life, drawing upon original news reports and witness recollections. All quotations from news articles and eyewitnesses to Julia's life are likewise taken from the same work. Since all other published books and recent articles on Greeley draw upon Father Burkey's research, there is no need to use additional sources.

good deeds away from public view, although that is true. I mean that, beyond consciously seeking to avoid attracting attention to herself, she bore the cross of social invisibility.

Most if not all of us have felt socially invisible at some point in life. Even in our present egalitarian age, in certain environments women continue to suffer social invisibility compared to men, and older women are particularly likely to be ignored. The disabled also suffer such invisibility, as do the poor, the uneducated, and those whose appearance is deemed unattractive. And, in predominantly white areas of the United States, African Americans can feel uniquely invisible, being treated by their white neighbors as anonymous "others."

Julia Greeley, as a poor, uneducated, disfigured, and physically disabled older Black woman, lived a unique level of social invisibility. Yet, however invisible she may have been to her Denver neighbors, she was glorious in the sight of God as she gave herself fully to spreading devotion to the Sacred Heart and doing works of charity for the city's poor.

Only in death did Julia's stunningly important role in her community—an overwhelmingly white city where African Americans made up only 2 percent of the population—become visible to all. When her body was laid out for viewing at Sacred Heart Parish's Loyola Chapel, so many people swarmed the small building that the pastor permitted the wake to continue for five hours. As local and national newspapers would report, it was the first time in Denver Catholic history (and perhaps even US Catholic history) that a layperson was granted the honor of lying in state. Four days later, the *Denver Catholic Register* reported on its front page:

How in the world all the people learned of her death and of the fact that she was to lie in state is astonishing. The fact that the news spread so quickly, without the assistance of the printed word, is proof of the great love which the Denver public had for this quaint and saintly old character. . . . Limousines and giant touring cars came carrying the rich to see her. The poor flocked to the chapel in throngs.

Likewise, the *Register* added, the following day, at Julia's funeral Mass at Sacred Heart Church, "the prosperous and the poor, the educated and the uneducated, the prominent and the unknown were there."

What did Julia do with her life that led such crowds to stream to her viewing, learning about it only through word of mouth? Given her popularity, the answer to that question is more difficult to ascertain than one might expect.

During the years after Julia's death, several people attempted to collect reminiscences from those whose lives she touched. Although ultimately enough evidence of Julia's sanctity was collected to fulfill the requirements to open her cause for canonization, very few people came forth with substantial recollections. Among those few was Eleanor Pavella Castellan, who was thirty when Julia died. Decades later, she sought out others whom she hoped might be able to augment her memories of her holy friend, but her efforts came up short. "I called many people who knew her," Castellan wrote in 1969, "and they would always say, 'Yes, I knew Julia, but I don't remember anything about her.'"

It seems, then, that many of those who showed up at Julia Greeley's funeral likely did so not because of what she did—for they didn't know the details of her life or good works. They showed up because of who she was. Even those who knew her only by sight recognized that Julia radiated the love of the Sacred Heart of Jesus.

Although Julia did not enter the Catholic Church until adulthood, in some way she bore the cross her entire life. She was born into slavery in Hannibal, Missouri, in the 1830s or 1840s. A woman of dignity, she normally demurred when asked her age. However, when pressed, she would admit that she did not know her exact year of birth. When Julia was three, the whip of a cruel slaveowner destroyed the vision in her right eye. It is thought that the whip might have been intended for her mother; Julia could have been trying to protect her mother or hiding behind her. For the rest of Julia's life, tear fluid would flow continually from the area of her damaged eye. Those who knew her in Denver, when she was an adult, recall that she had to constantly wipe her eye with a handkerchief.

Julia was middle-aged and, since being freed under the Emancipation Proclamation, had been working as a domestic servant when, in the late 1870s, she moved from Missouri to Denver on the promise of employment in the home of a local married couple, William and Julia Gilpin. It was through the influence of Mrs. Gilpin, a prayerful Catholic, that Julia Greeley was moved to enter the Catholic Church herself on June 26, 1880, at Sacred Heart Catholic Church, Denver's first Jesuit parish, which had been dedicated just two months earlier.

At her reception into the Catholic Church, Julia was conditionally baptized, as it was not known whether she had received baptism as an infant. But there was no doubt in her mind that her life in Christ began with her Catholicism. Later on, when somebody said to her of the Gilpins, "They ought to leave you a little money," Julia replied, "They've given me more than money— they gave me my faith."

For a time after her conversion, Julia remained employed by the Gilpins. However, William Gilpin, who was not Catholic, developed an irrational hostility toward Julia. In particular, he resented the warm affection that his wife and children had for her. By the spring of 1883, he had not only fired her but also had begun a rumor campaign accusing her of immorality, intending to prevent her from finding employment elsewhere.

As Julia struggled to find steady work, the Gilpins' marriage deteriorated. In 1887, William Gilpin sued for divorce, packing his brief with two dozen accusations against his wife, many of them outrageous. Included among them was the claim that she had brought "a lewd and unprincipled woman" into the home— meaning Julia Greeley.

Many people testified on Julia's behalf at the divorce trial, calling her a good servant of high character, modesty, and virtue. A century later, such testimony would prove extremely valuable for those seeking to promote Julia's canonization. But, from Julia's perspective, the trial must have been a nightmarish experience, as both her own reputation and Mrs. Gilpin's, whom she loved dearly, were attacked.

The Gilpins' divorce case dragged on through the courts for four years, affording Julia a new level of identification with the suffering Christ. Julia had known suffering from childhood, enduring scourging as a slave, as well as other abuses as a servant under William Gilpin. But with her firing, William Gilpin's ensuing rumors, and the court case, Julia endured additional kinds of blows in line with those Jesus endured in his Passion: unjust public accusations and mockery. Like her divine master, she was persecuted for the sake of righteousness.

Yet, Julia is not being considered for sainthood for her suffering, but rather for how she responded to it. Instead of sinking into bitterness and isolation, she entered more deeply into her relationship with God. This intimate relationship manifested itself in her devotion to the Sacred Heart of Jesus, and, through it, in three areas of apostolic works that she accomplished in the heart of her local community: prayer, evangelization, and acts of charity.

Given the name of the parish where she was received, it is not surprising that Julia developed a devotion to the Sacred Heart. But the depth of her devotion to the Sacred Heart (as well as to the Virgin Mary and the Blessed Sacrament), and the lengths she went to share it with others, impressed even the parish's Jesuits, whose mission was to promote it. "It was not sentimentality, but real piety," said Sacred Heart associate pastor Father Charles A. McDonnell, SJ.

At some point after her conversion to Catholicism, Julia joined the Apostleship of Prayer, a fellowship sponsored by the Society of Jesus that was then popularly known as the League of the Sacred Heart. The Apostleship of Prayer promotes a robust understanding of the Sacred Heart as the way each member of the faithful enters into union of prayer with both Jesus and the church at large. It does this primarily by encouraging members to pray a daily offering each morning.

The morning offering recommended by the Apostleship of Prayer in Julia's time went, "O Jesus, through the Immaculate Heart of Mary, I offer thee my prayers, works, and sufferings of this day for all the intentions of thy Sacred Heart, in union with the holy sacrifice of the Mass throughout the world, for the intentions of all our Associates, and in particular for . . ."—here the person praying would insert the pope's prayer intention for the month. Although the "thee" and "thy" show the prayer's age (its language has since been updated), the idea behind the morning offering was remarkably forward-thinking for its time. Decades before Vatican II's teachings affirmed the laity's call to holiness, the Apostleship of Prayer was urging every Catholic to reflect upon the incalculable value that their ordinary daily activities had when united to Christ's sacrifice made present in the Mass.

Julia couldn't have known it, but at about the same time that she joined the Apostleship of Prayer, a young girl living on the other side of the Atlantic Ocean who was praying the same morning offering would become a great saint of the church.

Twelve-year-old Thérèse Martin—St. Thérèse of Lisieux—joined the Apostleship in October 1885. Its morning offering shaped her prayer life in much the way that it did Julia's. In her autobiography *Story of a Soul*, Thérèse would write that the purpose of her life was "to be a daughter of the Church . . . and to pray for the Holy Father's intentions which I know embrace the whole universe." That purpose, Thérèse went on, enabled her to reach out in apostolic work, which for her—since she was by then a cloistered Carmelite nun—meant praying for seminarians and priests being sent to the missions.[2]

Julia too felt that Jesus's Sacred Heart willed that she help people who were putting themselves in danger for the good of others. But whereas Thérèse's call was to encourage men who, by God's grace, were working to save souls, Julia felt compelled to reach out to those working to save lives. Although she earned only either fifty cents or a dollar a day (which was minimal even in the early twentieth century), each year Julia purchased fifty subscriptions of the Apostleship of Prayer newsletter, *Messenger of the Sacred Heart*, as well as two hundred Catholic almanacs. Then, in advance of the first Friday of each month (the day the church celebrates the First Friday devotion to the Sacred Heart), she would personally deliver those publications and other Catholic literature to every firehouse in Denver. She also carried small badges made of felt and paper that displayed an image of the Sacred Heart, which she likely had a priest bless so that the person who carried one in faith on his person would receive special graces from God.

---

2. St. Thérèse of Lisieux, *Story of a Soul: The Autobiography of St. Thérèse of Lisieux*, 2nd ed., trans. John Clarke (Washington: ICS Publications, 1976), 253–54.

Since the city was spread out, with more than a dozen fire-houses (twenty by the time of Julia's death), reaching every station required that Julia—old, half-blind, and crippled by arthritis—walk twenty-two miles with her large, heavy black handbag. When she arrived at each firehouse, she would give literature and a badge to each fireman and say, "God bless you all." Eleanor Pavella Castellan recalled, "The men would joke with her and tease her, but she would just laugh and go on her way." Although not all the firemen were Catholic, "it made no difference to her" when she went on her monthly rounds. "She would always say, 'They are all God's children.'"

The firemen were far from the only beneficiaries of Julia's charity. Over time, she made a life for herself akin to that of St. Elizabeth of Hungary, who seems to have been a model for her; she took St. Elizabeth's name for her vow name when, in 1901, she was received into the Third Order of St. Francis (today known as the Secular Franciscan Order). But whereas St. Elizabeth of Hungary began her service to the poor while she was wealthy and in a high position, Julia began hers while at her lowest ebb since gaining her freedom, having been fired and defamed. Truly, her gift of self was the widow's mite of which Jesus spoke (Mark 12:41–44).

Most of the recorded recollections of Julia were collected by a Franciscan priest, Father Pacificus Kennedy, OFM, in the 1970s. Neil Horan, a Denver resident who was in his late teens when

Julia died, wrote to Kennedy that, as far as he could tell, when Julia wasn't mopping the floor of Sacred Heart Church (for which she was paid), she was collecting and distributing clothes for the poor. "I have a very vivid boyhood recollection of [Julia]," Horan said, adding:

> I went to old Sacred Heart School and Church and over the years on my way to either place, I would meet Julia pulling a little red wagon loaded with clothes that she had collected.
>
> Some times she would greet me with 'Hello, Sonny,' and a few cheery remarks. Other times she would have a little black book and she and the wagon would be stopped in front of a house where she had made a collection. Then she would say, 'Sonny, would you please write that number (pointing to the number of the house) in this book—I left my glasses at home and I can't see too well without them.' I was always happy to comply—I doubt if she could write, even if she could see. . . .
>
> She never seemed to use any of the clothes for herself. The old clothes she wore were always the same.

What stood out to Horan most was Julia's joy. "God must have loved her greatly," he observed, "because in her poverty she was always happy, seeking only to help others whom she considered less fortunate than herself. It was incongruous to see that lovely smile while a tear dropped from her poor blind eye." Many others were similarly struck by Julia's radiant demeanor. Mildred Connell Arkins, who was barely ten when Julia died, told Father Kennedy, "What I remember most is how her face always glowed."

In fact, Julia was never happier than when around children. Sometimes, as Eleanor Pavella Castellan recalled, she would arrange a picnic for them at City Park, a grand green space that was conceived along the lines of New York City's Central Park:

> She would round up as many as she could at one time (nine or ten) and would take them on the trolley car. Of course she always joshed with the conductor that they were all her children. I remember because I was one of them. We each had a nickel or a dime to spend, and Julia always provided and brought along lunch for all of us. We would come home happy and tired, Julia the happiest of all because she had spent the day with the children.

Something of the joy Julia felt around children comes through in the lone existing photograph of her. She faces the camera with a smile, wearing her trademark floppy black hat and a light-colored summer dress as she holds a seven-month-old blonde girl whose fingers clutch what appears to be a rosary. The child pictured in it, Marjorie Ann Urquhart, preserved the photo and later wrote to Father Kennedy about how Julia came to befriend her mother.

Marjorie reported that her mother Agnes told her that, one day in 1914, Julia was walking past the Urquhart home as Agnes sat in a rocking chair on the front porch. Julia must have looked like she was in need of work, or perhaps Agnes had seen her doing cleaning elsewhere, for Agnes called out to ask if she would mop their kitchen floor.

When Julia entered the house, she noticed holy pictures on the walls (probably of the Sacred Heart and the Immaculate Heart) and a crucifix. "You must be a Catholic," Julia said. "Why aren't there any little children running around this house?" Agnes replied sadly that her only child, a boy, had died in infancy more than ten years earlier, and she was no longer capable of having children. But Julia saw a different future for Agnes and her husband. "There will be a little white angel running around this house," she said. "I will pray and you'll see."

And so it happened; Marjorie was born the following year. The Urquharts employed Julia to help care for the little girl, who loved her intensely. When Julia would arrive in the morning, Marjorie would eagerly hug her and shower her face with kisses.

Not every child who wished to be close to Julia was permitted to do so. Katie Laetitia Taylor, who later took the name Sister Catherine Regina as a Sister of Charity, wrote to Father Kennedy that she wanted one of the holy cards that Julia gave to children whom she sponsored for confirmation. So she told her mother that she wanted Julia for her own sponsor because she was holy. "I don't care how holy she is," Katie's mother replied. "You're not going to have a colored woman for a sponsor."

Julia did not let such prejudice prevent her from engaging in acts of generosity toward those who needed them. Newspaper reports at the time of her death noted the care she took to protect the pride of poor white families whom she helped, who could lose what little social status they had if they were seen receiving assistance from a Black woman. Castellan later collected stories exemplifying Julia's discretion:

> When a new baby arrived for a poor family that had no baby buggy, Julia would scout around and find a family that had a used baby carriage and no baby in prospect. She would deliver at night when nobody could see her.

Julia put a sack of potatoes on the porch of a poor family right in front of the door. She watched from across the street unobserved. It was very cold—nobody came out of that door. Julia was afraid the potatoes would freeze and get mushy, [so] she went next door and got a little child to ring the doorbell—"But don't dast say that Old Julia had anything to do with it."

Another object of Julia's charity was Sacred Heart Church itself. Although the church had many wealthy parishioners, Julia was its most active fundraiser—and likely its most creative one as well. Once, the parish's Young Ladies Sodality held a benefit in the form of a popularity/beauty contest, charging ten cents per vote. Julia was willing to take the risk of being teased by going to the city's firemen and asking them to vote for her. She raised about $350—and won the contest.

Julia was a daily communicant at Sacred Heart, seating herself at one of the pews closest to the communion rail on the church's left-hand side. The pew was made to seat two persons; Julia chose it so she could take up the least amount of space, since it was certain that none of the other parishioners, all of whom were white, would sit next to her.

Despite Julia's efforts to maintain some distance between herself and others at Mass, there were parishioners who were scandalized by her presence. "Some of the wealthy used to bring their friends to high Mass—for the music," Castellan recalled. "Let's face it, Julia could look pretty tacky in her hand-me-downs, and she had big feet and shoes that hardly fit, and she would be flopping them up the aisle." But when the offended parishioners complained about her presence to the pastor, Father Edward D. Barry, SJ, "He said emphatically, 'As long as I'm pastor here, Julia is going to keep her pew.'" When word of the complaint reached Julia, she approached Father Barry and offered to attend a different Mass. But the pastor insisted she keep her regular seat because he knew how much she wished to attend high Mass. In time, he even placed her name on the pew, marking it just as pews were marked for wealthy parishioners who could afford to reserve their own seats.

Around dawn on the morning of June 7, 1918, Julia was walking from her boarding-house room to Sacred Heart when she fell ill. She knocked on the door of a female friend who quickly sent her daughter to Sacred Heart to fetch a priest. Sacred Heart associate pastor Father Charles A. McDonnell, SJ, was able to reach Julia in time to administer the final sacraments. He then saw to it that Julia was admitted to a local Catholic hospital, St. Joseph's, which normally refused to treat African Americans.

Julia breathed her last at midnight—just as the Feast of the Sacred Heart, her parish's patronal feast day, was coming to a close. The *Denver Catholic Register* expressed the thoughts of many when it reported, "The time of her death, considering the work she did in life, makes it look as if the very finger of God was present." Having given her life in service to her neighbors, never holding onto resentment, but going the extra mile to be present for people in need of human kindness, she died the way she lived, in the Heart of Jesus.

Chapter Seven

The Heart of Sacrifice

St. Tarcisius, St. Juliana Falconieri, and
Catherine de Hueck and Eddie Doherty

———————◆———————

There is one aspect of the spirituality of the Sacred Heart that has
been an undercurrent throughout this book, and it is time now
to bring it to the surface. It is what theologians call nuptiality, or
nuptial spirituality, and it is too large a topic for us to limit our
examples of it to just one saint.

By nuptial spirituality, I don't mean experiences of mystical
marriage to Jesus, such as those reported by St. Margaret Mary
Alacoque and St. Faustina Kowalska. What I mean is something
that everyone who believes in God—even non-Catholics—is
capable of experiencing. Nuptial spirituality at its core is simply
a way of understanding the soul's relationship to God as a kind
of marital union. Just as, in marriage, spouses vow themselves
to each other and commit to living a common life as long as
they both shall live, so too, in nuptial spirituality, do the faithful
understand themselves to be inseparably joined to God, sharing

their lives with him. Admittedly, there is more to it than that: God, unlike a human spouse, created us, knows us better than we know ourselves, and is always and everywhere worthy of our complete obedience and trust.

What does nuptial spirituality have to do with the Sacred Heart? The answer is "quite a lot" if we think of nuptial spirituality the way St. Paul does in Ephesians 5:21–33. In those verses, Paul paints a verbal image of Christ's love for the church as the model for how husbands and wives should love one another. Here are three things he emphasizes about the spousal nature of Jesus's love:

1. ***Jesus "handed himself over" to death for the church* (Ephesians 5:25).** This fact is certainly no surprise to anyone who has read the Gospels. But it is significant within the context of nuptial spirituality because it emphasizes Jesus's gift of self. It is in the nature of spousal love for a husband and wife to give themselves over to one another, each sacrificing for the other. The greater the goodness of the spouse who is giving, the more sincere is the gift. To borrow a phrase from Vatican II, Jesus, who is perfectly good, makes a perfectly "sincere gift of himself,"[1] setting a model for spouses and, most importantly, a model for our own spousal love toward God.

---

1. Second Vatican Council, Pastoral Constitution on the Church in the Modern World Gaudium et spes, §22, https://www.vatican.va/archive/hist_councils/ii_vatican_council/documents/vat-ii_cons_19651207_gaudium-et-spes_en.html.

2. ***Jesus wants us to be capable of returning his love—and he equips us to do so* (Ephesians 5:26–27).** A moving moment in the musical *Jesus Christ Superstar* (in good productions of it, anyway) is when Mary Magdalene sings, "I Don't Know How to Love Him." The character speaks in some way for all of us. We don't know how to love Jesus—at least, not as we should. If God left us to our own powers, we would be utterly incapable of reaching out to him. Thankfully, God does not leave us to our own powers. Through the sanctifying grace that Jesus won for us on the cross, he gives us the love that empowers us to love him.[2]

3. ***Jesus loves us as his own Body* (Ephesians 5:28–33).** Here we have the crux of the matter. Just as a husband and wife become "one flesh" (Matthew 19:5)—an expression that refers not so much to their sexual relations as it does to their entire communion of life—so too does Jesus, having united us to him through the waters of baptism, recognizes us as members of his own Body.

When I think of this amazing truth of the Catholic faith, I think of the title of Clarence Enzler's spiritual classic that is written from the perspective of Jesus: *My Other Self.*[3] Aristotle, in his *Nicomachean Ethics*, speaks of a friend as being another self.[4]

---

2. See *Catechism*, §§2000–2002.

3. See Clarence Enzler, *My Other Self* (Notre Dame, IN: Christian Classics, 2020).

4. Aristotle, *Nicomachean Ethics*, bk. 9, chapter 4.

From Christ's perspective, each one of us is another self, for he is our truest friend—the friend with love so great that he gave his life for us (John 15:13). And marriage is, in the words of St. Thomas Aquinas, the greatest kind of friendship.[5]

Taken together, these three elements of the nuptial spirituality that Paul describes in Ephesians 5 help us purify our understanding of nuptiality as it applies to our relationship with God. Paul writes earlier in Ephesians that God's fatherhood is the model for all human parenthood (see Ephesians 3:15). So too Jesus's marriage to the church—and, by extension, to the soul of every Christian—is the model of all human marriage. Yet, because we human persons[6] can never live up to our divine blueprint, when we contemplate our union with Christ, we need to remove from our imagination everything that is sinful, or is a consequence of original sin, or is something that applies only to our life here on earth.[7]

Once we have succeeded in purifying our understanding of nuptiality from those things that don't apply to union with Christ, what remains? For the Christian, the answer to that question is to be lived rather than explained. But since God made us rational creatures who want to get to the bottom of things, there is no stopping theologians and spiritual authors from trying to explain it.

---

5. Thomas Aquinas, *Summa contra gentiles* 3b.123.6.

6. Whenever you see me make broad generalizations such as this about human persons, unless otherwise noted, please insert the mental note, "except for the Blessed Virgin Mary."

7. The church's theological authorities hold that sexual intercourse falls into that last category. Here on earth, its purpose is to procreate life and to unite married couples more closely. Neither purpose remains in heaven, where the saints' joyful experience of union with Christ is on a level beyond any earthly joy.

To me (and if I claimed this idea was original, every institution that has awarded me a theology degree would revoke it),[8] nuptial spirituality is the union between Jesus and the individual Christian as experienced through baptism; the sacraments; prayer and its fruits in everyday life; and, especially, reception of the Eucharist. Through our sacramental union with Christ, we are one flesh with him, and he lives with us in a true communion of life.

To take that idea to its logical conclusion, nuptial spirituality is, in a sense, the living out of each Christian's experience of being transubstantiated into the Body of Christ. In our earthly life, we experience only the beginning of this transubstantiation. It takes place in our soul, not in our body, which is still subject to suffering and death (though our body can feel the effects of spiritual joy and can act on Christ's behalf). But in heavenly life after the general resurrection, even though we will retain our personhood (as Jesus promises when he speaks of the "many dwelling places" he has prepared for us [John 14:2–3]), our material body will be transformed into a spiritual one incapable of suffering.[9]

I have in mind what St. Thomas Aquinas describes when he likens the effect of transubstantiation upon bread and wine (which, through the Holy Spirit's power and Jesus's words of consecration voiced by the priest, become Christ's Body and Blood)

---

8. I hold graduate degrees in theology from the Pontifical Faculty of the Immaculate Conception at the Dominican House of Studies in Washington, DC, and from the University of St. Mary of the Lake in Mundelein, Illinois. In addition, I have a license in canon law from the Catholic University of America, but don't let anyone try to fool you into thinking that canon lawyers necessarily know theology (though many would like you to think so). You might as well expect them to know how to fix your sink.

9. See St. Paul's reflections on the resurrected body in 1 Corinthians 15:35–58.

to that of the Eucharist upon the faithful. "It was fitting," Thomas writes, "that this sacrament, in which the incarnate Word is contained in order to unite us to himself, be proposed to us under the figure of food, not so that he may be converted into us by his union with us, but rather so that, by our union with Him, we may be converted into him."[10]

When I seek a deeper understanding of what it means to be transformed by Jesus's nuptial love, I look to the lives of saints who gave a full-bodied "yes" to such transformation. All saints have given such a "yes," but some have done so in more dramatic fashion than others. They have lived remarkably sacrificial lives in imitation of Jesus's own sacrifice of himself on the cross that he presents anew to us through the Eucharist.

Since that "yes" looks different for each person according to their circumstances and state of life (such as whether they are married or single), I would like here to look at the lives of four holy people who each sought in their own way to imitate the nuptial love of the Heart of Jesus: the Roman martyr St. Tarcisius, the medieval religious sister St. Juliana Falconieri, and the twentieth-century married couple Catherine de Hueck and Eddie Doherty.

---

10. Thomas Aquinas, *Sentences* 4.8.1.3.1, quoted in Giles Emery, "The Ecclesial Fruit of the Eucharist in St. Thomas Aquinas," *Nova et Vetera*, Eng. ed., vol. 2, no. 1 (2004): 47.

St. Tarcisius: Made One with Christ

We know very little about St. Tarcisius. What we do know is written on his tomb in the Catacombs of St. Callixtus, inscribed by Pope Damasus I in the late 300s, telling us that Tarcisius's martyrdom likely occurred a century earlier, during the Roman emperor Valerian's persecution of Christians. Although he is popularly depicted as a child acolyte who was martyred by young bullies, modern scholars believe he was probably a young deacon martyred by Roman soldiers, as Damasus's inscription likens him to the deacon St. Stephen, the first martyr.

With that said, the pious legends and contemporary scholarship both agree on what Tarcisius was doing when he was martyred. Whether he was a child or an adult, we know that Tarcisius's attackers suspected—correctly—that a priest had given him the Eucharist to deliver to a Christian community. When his attackers demanded he surrender the Eucharist, he refused to do so.

But Tarcisius's death was not the end of the story. *The Roman Martyrology* tells us that his pagan killers turned over his corpse, searching vainly for the Blessed Sacrament. Once they realized that the sacrament was not on his person, they became seized with fear and fled, abandoning his body where it lay on the Appian Way. The belief emerged among Christians that, in the moment that Tarcisius sacrificed himself to prevent the Eucharist from being profaned by his attackers, the Body of Christ became one with his own body.

In the words of Pope Benedict XVI, "the consecrated Host which the little Martyr had defended with his life, had become flesh of his flesh thereby forming, together with his body, a single immaculate Host offered to God."[11] It was a literal representation of the "great mystery" that St. Paul describes in Ephesians 5:32, the reality of which human marriage symbolizes, by which Christ becomes one flesh, one body, with his Church.

St. Juliana Falconieri: Accompanied into Heaven

St. Juliana Falconieri was born to a devout and noble family in Florence in 1270 (which makes her a near contemporary of fellow Florentine Dante Alighieri).[12] Her father built the city's Church of the Santissima Annunziata, and her uncle was the priest known today as St. Alexis Falconieri, one of the seven founders of the Servite Order, which promoted devotion to Jesus's Passion and to the Seven Sorrows of the Blessed Virgin Mary.[13]

When Juliana approached the age of fourteen—the age at which a young woman became marriageable in medieval Florence—her mother sought to have her wed a wealthy young man. Juliana, however, who had placed herself under the spiritual guidance of Father Alexis, resisted being married to the youth—or

---

11. Benedict XVI, "Saint Tarcisius," speech, General Audience, August 4, 2010, St. Peter's Square, Vatican City, https://www.vatican.va/content/benedict-xvi/en/audiences/2010/documents/hf_ben-xvi_aud_20100804.html.

12. Johann Peter Kirsch, "St. Juliana Falconieri," in *The Catholic Encyclopedia*, vol. 8 (New York: Robert Appleton Co., 1910), https://www.newadvent.org/cathen/08556a.htm.

13. Frederick W. Faber, ed., *The Lives of St. Rose of Lima, the Blessed Colomba of Rieti, and of St. Juliana Falconieri* (London: Thomas Richardson and Son, 1847), 357. Unless otherwise noted, details of Juliana's life are from Faber's account.

to anyone, for she sought to be espoused to Christ alone. Instead, she agreed to have Father Alexis present her to the Servites' General Superior, St. Philip Benizi, who, in 1284, inducted her as the first member of what would become the Servites' female branch, the Sisters of the Third Order of Servites.[14]

Juliana and other young women who followed her into the Third Order wore dark cloaks like those of the Servite Fathers, and thus were known as *Mantellate*, which means "cloaked." (Third Order Dominican women of the time such as St. Catherine of Siena received the same nickname.) After the Servites clothed her in the cloak, she reported to her spiritual director that she felt joy and also a kind of mystically induced pain, as she identified herself deeply with the crucified Christ.

In addition to her mystical pain, Juliana also submitted herself to the kind of extreme personal deprivations and other physical penances that we commonly find in the lives of saints, especially medieval ones. Although extreme penances are thankfully no longer permitted in religious life (and even back then were often discouraged by spiritual directors and religious superiors concerned for the health of their charges), it is important to understand them within the context of the time. Medieval Florence was subject to violence between elite members of various clans that considered carrying out vendettas to be a duty of honor.[15] Juliana and her sisters in the Mantellate offered to God

---

14. Faber, *The Lives*, 365–66; "St. Juliana Falconieri, Virgin, Foundress of the Mantellate," *Vatican News*, https://www.vaticannews.va/en/saints/06/19/st--juliana-falconieri--virgin--foundress-of-the--mantellate.html.

15. See Peter W. Sposato, *Forged in the Shadow of Mars: Chivalry and Violence in Late Medieval Florence* (Ithaca, NY: Cornell University Press), 2022.

their personal sacrifices to call down divine grace for conversion and peace. They stood out in their scandal-ridden city as a sign of contradiction.

Although Juliana practiced heroic virtue during her active life, including caring for the sick, her sanctity was displayed most dramatically at the moment of her death on June 19, 1341.[16] She was seventy-one and had become so ill from her fasting and penances that she could no longer keep food down.[17] When her doctors determined that the end was near, although she was joyful at the prospect of heaven, at the same time she grieved that, due to her nausea, final Communion was out of the question. As she lay dying, Juliana ardently begged the Servite Third Order's director, Father Giacomo, that she might at least see the Blessed Sacrament before her death, and she kept on begging until he finally acceded.

As Father Giacomo brought the Host into her room, Juliana tried several times to get up from her sickbed. Finally, she succeeded in prostrating herself upon the floor in the form of a cross. Juliana then returned to her bed and, crying, begged to be permitted to kiss the Host. A priest today might be willing to accommodate such a request for a desperately ill patient, even if he then had to dispose of the Host in a manner permitted by the church. But in Juliana's time, there were restrictions against nonordained people handling the Eucharist in any way unless they were consuming it.

---

16. Although Faber, who adapted an eighteenth-century life of the saint, wrote that Juliana was seventy-four when she died, I am using the date given on the Servite Order's website, which states that she died at seventy-one in 1341.

17. Faber, *The Lives*, 382.

Even so, Juliana managed to convince Father Giacomo to take the extraordinary measure of placing a corporal—the sacred cloth that is normally used on the altar at Mass—upon her chest and, upon it, placing the Host. After the priest did so, Juliana died—and those present were astonished to see that the Host had vanished.

It remained for Juliana's fellow Third Order sisters to lay out her body and wash it in preparation for burial. When they did, they discovered something that they deemed miraculous: a small cross on the skin of her chest. It was just beneath where the Host had lain, and indeed it resembled the cross that had been on the Host. As with St. Tarcisius, the conclusion drawn by the faithful, and affirmed by the church in canonizing Juliana, was that the eucharistic Christ had, in the words of one writer, "accompanied her to heaven."[18] It was Jesus's way of acknowledging that Juliana in her death was so close to him as to be truly another self.

Catherine de Hueck and Eddie Doherty: United in the Sacred Heart

Six centuries separate Juliana Falconieri from Catherine de Hueck and Eddie Doherty, but the Dohertys' lives are so different from Juliana's that they seem an entire universe apart. Yet, if we look at how they grew in their relationship with God and with each other, we will find a profound similarity between their spirituality and that of Juliana and Tarcisius, even though—spoiler alert!— no more eucharistic miracles await us in this chapter.

---

18. Faber, *The Lives*, 386.

Catherine, whose cause has been introduced for sainthood (currently she is called a Servant of God), was born Ekaterina Katya Kolyschkine in 1896 into a noble family in what was then Tsarist Russia and was baptized in the Russian Orthodox Church.[19] At fifteen, she married her first cousin Boris de Hueck, a twenty-two-year-old who was likewise of noble stock and had income from an inheritance. Although Boris was charming while courting Catherine, after the wedding he became verbally and emotionally abusive. Catherine would later say that her parents pressured her to marry Boris after they saw that she was besotted with him. "My life can be divided into two parts," she said. "Up to my marriage, it was heaven. After my marriage, it was hell."[20]

Despite her wealthy background, Catherine, inspired by the life of St. Francis of Assisi, felt drawn from a young age to give of her own resources to help the poor. She also had a strong personal relationship with God, which grew as she encountered the horrors of war during World War I, when she served as a Red Cross nurse on the front while her husband was fighting in the Russian Army.

When the Bolshevik Revolution swept Russia in 1917, Catherine and Boris sought safety at her parents' summer home in Finland. Finnish Bolsheviks, however, found them there and

---

19. My main source for information on the Dohertys is Lorene Hanley Duquin, *They Called Her the Baroness* (Staten Island, NY: Alba House, 1995), but I am using the chronology provided in Donald A. Guglielmi, *Staritsa: The Spiritual Motherhood of Catherine Doherty* (Eugene, OR: Pickwick, 2018). Also consulted were Catherine Doherty, *Fragments of My Life* (Notre Dame, IN: Ave Maria Press, 1979); Eddie Doherty, *A Cricket in My Heart* (Combermere, ON: Madonna House Publications, 1990); and Echo Lewis, *Victorious Exile: The Unexpected Destiny of Katya Kolyschkine* (Combermere, ON: Madonna House Publications, 2013).

20. Duquin, *They Called Her the Baroness*, 29.

sentenced them to death by starvation. At some point over a period of several weeks, as Catherine and Boris were wasting away, Catherine made a promise to God that she would never forget: "If you save me from this, I will give my life to you."[21]

Catherine and Boris were indeed rescued, and, sixteen years later, in Toronto, Canada, Catherine began to make good on her promise to God. In 1933, she began to assemble a group of dedicated Catholic laypeople to join her in ministering to the poor. Together, the following year, they opened Friendship House, a place of hospitality—food, shelter, and, not least, Christian companionship—for those in need.

Much had changed in Catherine's life between her rescue and the beginning of her apostolate to the poor. Catherine had entered into full communion with the Catholic Church and had become involved in the Catholic Action movement—studying scripture, the saints, and papal encyclicals on social justice, and promoting a positive counter to communism through the teachings of the church. She also had become a mother to a son, George, born in 1921, a few months after she and Boris had arrived in Toronto. North Americans, impressed by Catherine's noble background and regal bearing, took to calling Catherine "the Baroness." The title stuck.

---

21. Guglielmi, *Staritsa*, 139.

Boris, however, remained as abusive as ever. Things came to a head when he began to openly carry on an affair with Claudia Kolenova, a Russian emigré and former ballet dancer whom Catherine had brought into their home to help care for George. In April 1930, Catherine received formal permission from her archbishop to separate from Boris, and she set the slow wheels of canonical justice turning to have her marriage declared null. (The church ultimately granted the annulment in March 1943 on the grounds that Catherine and Boris were first cousins and thus could not marry validly.)

In 1936, Friendship House ran into trouble due to false accusations of mismanagement and opposition from its parish priest, who felt it was not doing enough to combat communism. The apostolate was shut down by Toronto's bishop. Catherine, disconsolate, traveled to New York City to seek advice from her friend and mentor Dorothy Day, founder of the Catholic Worker apostolate (who, like Catherine, is now up for canonization).

Father John LaFarge, SJ, a Jesuit in the Catholic Worker's orbit who was a pioneer in interracial ministry, urged Catherine to restart Friendship House in Harlem. As Catherine meditated upon Father LaFarge's advice, she came to accept it as a genuine call, and in November 1938 the Blessed Martin de Porres Friendship House opened in a storefront on West 135th Street, named for a seventeenth-century Dominican lay brother of African descent.

As in Toronto, Catherine and her Harlem staff lived among the poor and ministered to their physical, psychological, and spiritual needs. To raise funds for the apostolate and raise awareness of those whom it served, Catherine also traveled to give lectures on the necessity for Catholics to fight communism through promoting Catholic social teaching, especially the church's teachings against racism. Typical of Catherine's lectures was one that she delivered in Boston just weeks after founding Friendship House Harlem. She told a packed, all-white audience at the Venetian Ballroom of the tony Copley Square Hotel (which, like every other major hotel in the city, refused service to African Americans): "There is no social justice without racial justice. We must not consider the Negro a case for charity, we must first give him justice. We must open jobs to those who very often are not only intellectually our equals but often our superiors."[22]

One day in September 1940, Eddie Doherty and Helen Worden, reporters from *Liberty*, one of the most popular weekly magazines in the country, came to Friendship House to seek out the Baroness. Their editor had assigned them to write a sensationalistic story on "Harlem, the Wickedest City in the World."

When Eddie saw Blessed Martin de Porres's name on the sign outside Friendship House, it gave him a start. Then as now, Blessed (now Saint) Martin wasn't a household name. But to Eddie he was a personal patron, for the reporter credited the holy Dominican with helping lead him back into the Catholic Church after a pair of tragedies. The first of those tragedies was the death of Eddie's first wife, Marie, in the 1918 flu pandemic, which left him having to raise their infant son on his own. In his sorrow,

22. "Russian Baroness Hits Communism," *Boston Globe*, November 21, 1938, 21.

Eddie turned away from the Catholic faith in which he had been raised. Then, in 1939, twenty-one years after losing Marie, Eddie suffered another terrible loss. His second wife, Mildred, died in a fall while walking alone on a hillside near a friend's home where the couple were staying. Five days after Mildred's funeral, Eddie, who had been edging back toward the Catholic faith, went to a priest for confession and returned to the bosom of the church.

In a memoir published after his death, *Cricket in My Heart*, Eddie wrote that, when he realized that Blessed Martin was Friendship House's patron, he thought, "Was it possible Blessed Martin also wanted to introduce me to the Baroness?"[23] But when he told Catherine why he and Worden were there, she was not amused. "I knew it!" Catherine shouted. "I knew it the moment you came through the door. I am sick and tired of reporters coming to me for filth."[24]

The Baroness went on for some time as Eddie and his fellow reporter stared. Eddie was stunned but also smitten. "Who made Harlem wicked, if it is wicked?" Catherine asked. And without waiting for an answer, she exclaimed, "Go ask City Hall. Go ask the respectable Christians of Manhattan and the Bronx, Catholics included. Go ask the landlords who gouge the people of Harlem. . . . Why don't you write about one of your Southern cities, if you want something really wicked?"[25]

To borrow a phrase from *Casablanca*, this was the beginning of a beautiful friendship. Eddie began to volunteer at Friendship

---

23. Doherty, *A Cricket in My Heart*, loc. 401, Kindle.

24. Doherty, *A Cricket in My Heart*, loc. 444, Kindle.

25. Doherty, *A Cricket in My Heart*, loc. 505, 533, Kindle.

House, where he delighted the local children by showing them his fancy red convertible. He could well afford it, for he was among the highest-paid reporters in the country. And he took Catherine out for meals, enjoying long conversations with her. However, as Eddie felt himself falling for Catherine, he learned from the longest-serving Friendship House staff member, Grace "Flewy" Flewelling—a woman who was, perhaps, a tad protective of the Baroness—that there was one thing he could not do: he could not ask her to marry him.

"Her spiritual director has forbidden her to marry," Flewy said. "She doesn't want to marry. She'd never dream of deserting us for any man. That would close Friendship House. That would be a tragedy. A tragedy, and a mortal sin!"[26]

But the prospect of Catherine being unattainable only made Eddie want to pursue her all the more. When, in October 1941, he moved back to his hometown of Chicago after being offered a position with the *Chicago Sun*, he schemed to bring Catherine to the city, where he hoped he could wear down her resistance to marriage. To that end, he spoke with Auxiliary Bishop Bernard Sheil, telling him of the good that Friendship House could do in the Chicago Archdiocese.

At first, it seemed that Eddie's plan was successful. Bishop Sheil agreed to meet with her while she was in town that December

---

26. Doherty, *A Cricket in My Heart*, loc. 1178, Kindle.

on a lecture tour. As Eddie and Catherine met with the bishop, he invited her to open a Friendship House in Chicago, and she immediately accepted.

There was just one catch: Bishop Sheil insisted that, as long as Catherine ran Friendship House, she must run it in complete freedom—which, he said, meant she must not marry. And Catherine accepted the bishop's dictum as the voice of God. Eddie was crushed. He felt he had been caught in his own trap. But, as disappointed as he was, he was determined not to give up.

And so, Catherine moved to Chicago, where Eddie continued to pursue her, now asking her to marry him. He asked her again and again, and her answer was always no. In her memoir *Fragments of My Life*, Catherine would recall, "I realized that if he married me, he would have to give up his whole life—his house, his job, his car."[27] Still, it pained Catherine to reject Eddie's proposals, for she was deeply attracted to him. "There was about him such an incredible gentleness that at first I could not quite understand it. No one (except my parents) had ever been that gentle with me."[28] Eddie's feelings for Catherine continued to grow as well, to the point where he found himself falling more deeply in love not only with her but also with the one great love of her life. He would later recall, "The closer I came to Catherine, the closer I came to the Lord, the closer I came to Catherine."[29]

In late March 1943, Catherine learned that the decree of nullity for her marriage to Boris had finally been granted. Eddie

27. Doherty, *Fragments of My Life*, 170.

28. Doherty, *Fragments of My Life*, 171.

29. Doherty, *A Cricket in My Heart*, loc. 1986, Kindle.

took the news—and its being granted on March 17, the Feast of St. Patrick, another of his patron saints—as a sign that he should renew his efforts to marry Catherine. This time, however, he wanted to have an audience—a very special audience.

Eddie managed to persuade Catherine to come with him to meet with Bishop Sheil on May 30 to ask him to reconsider his insistence that she not marry. Once they were in the room with the bishop, Eddie surprised Catherine by getting down on his knees to propose to her then and there. He offered to give up everything he owned, as well as his job, sharing in Catherine's poverty, so that Friendship House might always come first in her life. This time, the bishop gave his blessing. Appropriately, they married in June—the month of the Sacred Heart.

In her memoir, Catherine tells of the great joy that she felt in entering into married life with Eddie—a joy that flowed from their shared love of Jesus. Whenever they made love, they would complete the experience by going to Mass in the morning to receive Holy Communion together. "I began to feel the fullness of marriage in the sense that we were really one in Christ. Truly it was a wonderful realization."[30]

However, as Catherine and Eddie grew closer, tensions developed at Friendship House. Catherine had sought to be discreet about her marriage, but it wasn't long before the staff learned about it, and they felt betrayed. Although the staff ultimately came to accept Catherine's decision, other difficulties at Friendship House arose during the next few years, including differences of opinion over mission. In 1947, Catherine ended the

---

30. Doherty, *Fragments of My Life*, 171.

tensions by resigning from Friendship House and moving with Eddie to a house that they had purchased in rustic Combermere, Ontario, to start anew.

Once Catherine and Eddie settled in Combermere, they found a new direction for their apostolate. Instead of providing an oasis of hospitality in the inner city, they would provide a place of community and renewal for Catholics who sought to deepen their union with Jesus, Mary, and one another. In time, the apostolate became known as Madonna House. But before it could reach its full maturity, Catherine and Eddie were called to make a new sacrifice—and their greatest yet.

The decisive moment for the remainder of their life together came in late October 1951, in a café in Paris. Catherine and Eddie had gone to Rome together—he to research a book, she to attend a conference of leaders of lay apostolate. Since she needed to stay longer in the city than he did, they had agreed to reunite in Paris after the congress.

In a conversation that neither of them would ever forget, Catherine told Eddie that she had been called to meet with the pope's secretary of state, Monsignor Giovanni Montini (the future Pope Paul VI), and then with Pope Pius XII himself. Both were familiar with her apostolate, and both encouraged her to take it to a new level by making it a secular institute—a new form of religious life by which laymen and women could make and observe vows of poverty, chastity, and obedience while remaining laity. They would not have to wear religious habits, and they could continue their work in the world, sanctifying it from within.

Catherine's eyes and face were aglow as she spoke of having her life's work, her mission, affirmed by Pius XII. "The man is a living saint," she said, "a white flame of sanctity."[31]

But Eddie's thoughts lingered on the words "vows of . . . chastity." He realized what it would mean for him, for Catherine—for their marriage. And somehow, as shocking as it was, it was a cross that he felt was being offered to him from the hands of the Lord.

"My mind detoured back to Rome as Catherine talked," he later wrote, "back to early Rome, back to the days of the first Christians who died for Christ. . . . Catherine and I had been given a choice the early Christians never had. We could give up more than our lives. We could give not only ourselves; we could also give each other!"[32]

When his eyes again met Catherine's, he knew she was thinking the same thing.

"Each of us," Eddie wrote, "at the same time, had fallen on the sword of the holy will of God, and was stabbed with an unearthly joy!"[33] By the end of the conversation, he added, "There was not the slightest feeling of separation in either of us. Rather we felt closer together than we had when we sat down to eat and drink and talk. The swords had pinned us together, heart to heart, soul to soul, forever. How can a man explain such a thing?"

---

31. Doherty, *A Cricket in My Heart*, loc. 5093, Kindle.

32. Doherty, *A Cricket in My Heart*, loc. 5071–72, Kindle.

33. Doherty, *A Cricket in My Heart*, loc. 5108, Kindle.

What was happening, Eddie realized, was "something like what happened in the Crucifixion on Calvary. A soldier opened the dead Christ's heart with a lance, and it became a place of refuge for all the oppressed and hungry and desperate and despairing hearts in the world."[34] His and Catherine's hearts would be joined even more deeply not only with each other, but with all the Mystical Body, all who are united in and through the Heart of Jesus.

Catherine and Eddie continued to grow together with Jesus in a union of hearts, even as they lived in separate buildings within the Madonna House property. In time, Eddie would become Father Eddie, ordained in the Melkite Greek Catholic Church, which is in communion with Rome and permits married men to be ordained to the priesthood.

Shortly before his death in 1975, Eddie completed his memoir. It ends with a meditation on lyrics from the song "The Impossible Dream": "to love pure and chaste from afar . . . to reach the unreachable star." Eddie came to feel that, in learning to love Catherine purely and chastely from afar, he truly had reached the unreachable star. Through his sacrificial love for his wife, he had learned to love as Jesus loves.

Catherine outlived Eddie by a decade. In a talk she gave at a conference in 1979, she shared a reflection that revealed the depths of the intimacy that she felt both with Eddie and with

---

34. Doherty, *A Cricket in My Heart*, loc. 5071–72, Kindle.

God. The thought that came to her came as she sought to describe what it is like to "fall in love with God" in such a way that we become united with God and with one another in prayer, to the point of taking one another's burdens:

> Some of you are married; some of you know what it is to rest in the arms of a husband [or] a wife after the marriage act is consummated. Do you talk? No. I've been married twice.
>
> No, you don't talk. You lie in the arms of the beloved and you contemplate the lover, the beloved.
>
> Well, isn't that simple? That's what happens when prayer ceases to be a talk with God, even a meditation—when *you* become a prayer when you contemplate God, because he always contemplates you.[35]

Those final words remind me of 1 Peter 5:7, "Cast all your worries upon him"—Jesus—"because he cares for you." Tarcisius, Juliana, Catherine and Eddie—each in their own way suffered great hardship. But instead of folding in upon themselves, they accepted their trials as an opportunity to make a deeper gift of self to the Heart of Jesus. And when they, by the grace of God, drew nearer to him, he, like the true Bridegroom that he is, drew nearer to them.[36]

---

35. See Catherine de Hueck Doherty, "Sobornost—Catherine Doherty," speech, 1979, posted July 19, 2010, by Madonna House Apostolate, Youtube, 5 min., 37 sec., https://www.youtube.com/watch?v=_UYa81vgwtw.

36. See James 4:8.

Chapter Eight

The Heart of a Missionary

Father Pedro Arrupe, SJ

Speakers and authors discussing faith know that a surefire way to engage audiences is to illustrate ancient concepts by means of modern ones. St. Thérèse of Lisieux, when writing her spiritual memoir *Story of a Soul* in the mid-1890s, adopted that approach in a delightfully creative way, likening her "Little Way" of spiritual childhood to an invention that had only recently been patented: the electric elevator.

"We are living now in an age of inventions," the young Carmelite nun wrote, "and we no longer have to take the trouble of climbing stairs, for in the homes of the rich, an elevator has replaced these very successfully. I wanted to find an elevator that would raise me to Jesus, for I am too small to climb the rough stairway of perfection."[1] Thérèse went on to explain that, after

---

1. St. Thérèse of Lisieux, *Story of a Soul*, 207.

searching the Scriptures, she found that spiritual "elevator" in Jesus's arms. "And for this I had no need to grow up, but rather I had to remain *little* and become this more and more."[2]

Perhaps Father Pedro Arrupe, SJ, who, as a retreat master, promoted the Little Way, had Thérèse's writings in mind when he inserted a technological metaphor into a homily he delivered on May 8, 1970, on "What the Heart of Christ Means to the Society."

The society in question was the Society of Jesus. Arrupe, as Superior General, had a special interest both in reminding Jesuits what the Heart of Christ had historically meant to them and in encouraging them to reexamine its meaning. Many influential Catholics, both within and without the Society, had recently argued that Vatican II's liturgical reforms required that devotion to the Sacred Heart and other expressions of popular piety should be consigned to the past. Arrupe, acutely aware of such arguments, aimed with his homily to show that the present time—marked, in his words, "by chaotic confusion and at the same time by a cultural evolution"—desperately needed the love of Christ that is symbolized by his heart.[3]

The venue for Arrupe's homily, a shrine church in Valladolid, Spain, was uniquely appropriate for the message he intended to convey. In May 1733, when the church was the chapel of the Jesuit College of St. Ambrose, Bernardo de Hoyos, a Jesuit scholastic (that is, a seminarian) who had recently been asked by a

---

2. St. Thérèse of Lisieux, *Story of a Soul*, 208.

3. Pedro Arrupe, SJ, *In Him Alone Is Our Hope: Texts on the Heart of Christ* (Chestnut Hill, MA: Institute of Jesuit Sources, 2021), 8.

friend to translate a chapter from a Latin book on devotion to the Sacred Heart, had a mystical encounter with Jesus.[4] Bernardo told his spiritual director that Jesus wished him to spread devotion to the Sacred Heart throughout Spain. And, Bernardo said, Jesus promised that not only would the Sacred Heart come to reign in Spanish hearts, but that it would be venerated more intensely there than elsewhere. Although the young scholastic lived for only two and a half more years after the vision, he managed, with the help of several fellow Jesuits, to achieve amazing success in his mission. With Jesus's promise having been fulfilled, the church where Bernardo had his vision came to be renamed the Santuario Nacional de la Gran Promesa—the National Shrine of the Great Promise.

And so, Father Arrupe, in preaching to a group of Jesuits at Gran Promesa, chose like Thérèse to illustrate the power of the Heart of Christ with an electric image that was then in the headlines:

> Today, when so many new sources of energy are being discovered, when we stand amazed at all the triumphs of scientific research in atomic physics and in the energy of the atom that may transform the whole universe, we do not sufficiently realize that all human power and natural energy is nothing when compared with the super-atomic energy of this love of Christ, who by giving his life vivifies the world.[5]

---

4. My information on Bernardo de Hoyos, who was beatified (that is, made a Blessed of the Church, which is the last step before canonization) in 2010, is drawn from Hedwig Lewis, "Blessed Bernardo de Hoyos, SJ," accessed February 15, 2024, joygift.tripod.com/blessed_bernardo_model.htm.

5. Arrupe, *In Him Alone Is Our Hope*, 9.

Arrupe's comparison of the Sacred Heart with atomic energy no doubt captured his listeners' attention far more than it would have done coming from the lips of another priest. Those present knew that their Superior General, nearly a quarter-century earlier, had personally witnessed the destruction caused by the atomic bomb that the United States detonated over Hiroshima.

It was Father Arrupe's intense desire for union with the Heart of Christ that gave him strength as he ministered to victims of the Hiroshima attack. That desire began during his time in the Jesuit novice house in Loyola, Spain (on the grounds of Ignatius's ancestral estate), which he entered in 1927 at the age of nineteen. He had originally intended to become a doctor and had been a topflight medical student before he shocked his professors by quitting school to become a son of Ignatius.[6]

During the two-year novitiate, the new Jesuit becomes immersed in the spirituality of Ignatius of Loyola, the great sixteenth-century saint who founded the Society of Jesus. In addition to learning Ignatian practices of prayer and self-examination, each novice makes a thirty-day Spiritual Exercises retreat,

---

6. Unless otherwise noted, all biographical details about Father Arrupe are taken from the authoritative biography by Pedro Miguel Lamet, *Pedro Arrupe: Witness of the Twentieth Century, Prophet of the Twenty-First,* trans. Joseph V. Owens (Chestnut Hill, MA: Institute of Jesuit Sources, 2020).

meditating deeply upon sacred Scripture and salvation history according to Ignatius's guidelines. He will also read certain letters of Ignatius and study the Society's Constitutions.

The spirituality that Ignatius pioneered—particularly the Spiritual Exercises, with their focus on opening one's heart to God's love conveyed through Christ's humanity—lent itself naturally to the devotion to the Sacred Heart that began to take shape in the late 1600s. The Jesuits moreover felt a special responsibility to promote the Sacred Heart, given the pivotal role that one of their members, St. Claude La Colombière, had played in helping St. Margaret Mary Alacoque share her visions with the world. In the words of an 1883 decree by their General Congregation, they saw their role in spreading the devotion as a divinely given "*munus suavissismum*"—a "duty most sweet."

Arrupe became so attached to the Sacred Heart that, while still in the novitiate, he composed a booklet on the devotion.[7] A small number of copies of the booklet, typed and bound in simple gray cardboard under the title *El disco de Arrupe—Arrupe's Record*—came to be passed around among his fellow Jesuits. In it, Arrupe summarized authoritative sources concerning the origins of the devotion and its "tremendous importance." After examining the difficulties that some people encountered in practicing it, he concluded by showing how to attain and experience the devotion's true spirit. Although his devotion to the Sacred Heart would grow deeper over the course of his life (as would his understanding of it), he never lost his concern to help others overcome their obstacles to embracing it.

---

7. Lamet, *Pedro Arrupe*, 106.

Arrupe made his first vows in 1929 and entered the next stage of formation, known as the juniorate. Soon after, while making the required annual eight-day Spiritual Exercises retreat, he experienced what he would later call "the first sparks of my missionary vocation."[8] He felt certain that he was called to follow in the footsteps of the great Jesuit missionary St. Francis Xavier to win souls for Christ in Japan.

Although both the priest who directed Arrupe in his Spiritual Exercises and the rector of the juniorate believed his call was authentic, the decision of whether to send him to the Japanese missions lay with the Jesuit Superior General in Rome—and he did not feel the time was right. In fact, nearly ten years—and many more requests from Arrupe—would pass before the Society of Jesus's leader would finally grant Arrupe his heart's desire.

Father Arrupe had been ordained for two years when, in June 1938, the letter from Rome arrived calling him to undertake a missionary assignment in Japan. At the time, he was in Cleveland, Ohio, completing his final stage of Jesuit formation—the year of spiritual renewal known as tertianship. He arrived in the island nation in October 1938 and went to the Jesuit house of theology studies in Nagatsuka, where he entered into an intensive study of Japanese language and culture. Nagatsuka was on the outskirts of Hiroshima; a mountain separated it from the great city.

---

8. Lamet, *Pedro Arrupe*, 118.

After six months, the young priest felt confident enough in the local language to travel to Tokyo, where, as he would later write in his memoir, he hoped to enter into pastoral ministry. "I didn't know where to make a start," Arrupe recalled, "when Divine Providence put me on a path that I had only to follow."[9] The path opened up while Father Arrupe was visiting a community of religious sisters who told him they were having trouble finding a priest willing to take the time to consecrate their house to the Sacred Heart. Arrupe replied that if they could wait, he would gladly fulfill their request, for he would first need to prepare a consecration ceremony in Japanese.

True to his word, Arrupe wrote the act of consecration and some words of inspiration, and returned to lead the ceremony. It was then that he had an epiphany: "As long as I was stationed in Tokyo, I could dedicate myself to consecrate families to the Sacred Heart of Jesus."[10] The apostolate both suited his linguistic limitations and gave him a means of helping the small community of local Catholics, who had been evangelized by previous missionaries, to go deeper into their faith.

"I never regretted that step," Arrupe wrote.[11] He began by consecrating the homes of leading members of the community, and then word began to spread. Ultimately he consecrated more than one hundred homes to the Sacred Heart. Through such consecrations, he won many converts, including a Catholic woman's husband who was an adamant unbeliever and had resisted having any display of faith in the home.

---

9. Lamet, *Pedro Arrupe*, 99. I have tweaked the translation's grammar.

10. Lamet, *Pedro Arrupe*, 100.

11. Lamet, *Pedro Arrupe*, 100.

At the moment that the United States dropped the first of its atomic bombs upon Japan, at 8:15 a.m. Monday, August 6, 1945, Father Arrupe was meeting with another Jesuit in his office in Nagatsuka, where he was master of novices and vice rector at the house of studies. In his memoir, Arrupe described the shock they experienced: "That terrible force, which we thought would rip the building from its foundation, threw us to the ground."[12] They covered their heads with their hands as the walls and ceiling of the residence collapsed around them.

Once the dust began to clear, Arrupe and his friend arose, relieved to see that neither was injured. They then searched the rest of the building and found to their amazement that although the structure was severely damaged, none of the three dozen Jesuits there were wounded.

Arrupe's next thought was to check on the Jesuits who lived in the Society's residence in downtown Hiroshima, but he realized that was impossible, given the fire and black smoke rising from the city. So he carefully walked into what remained of the novitiate's chapel and took a few moments to call upon the Lord. "I left the chapel," Arrupe recalled afterwards, "and my decision was immediate. We would turn the house into a hospital."[13] Arrupe sent the Jesuit scholastics in search of food and other supplies that they would need to treat survivors. Injured people fleeing the city

---

12. Lamet, *Pedro Arrupe*, 263.

13. Lamet, *Pedro Arrupe*, 265.

soon began to arrive; within four and a half hours of the bomb blast, some one hundred and fifty wounded filled what was left of the house.

For many months, Father Arrupe devoted himself to treating the sick and injured. So great was his compassion—as well as the knowledge he retained from medical school—that he gained a reputation as a healer. At the same time, he did all that he could under the circumstances to maintain the ordinary life of the novitiate and house of studies. A novice who entered in early 1946 later recalled how "Father Arrupe worked at a truly exhausting pace. . . . He hardly had time to sleep. Despite that, he directed [the novices in] the monthlong [Spiritual] Exercises of St. Ignatius without leaving out a thing."[14]

By 1947, the remaining injured at the Jesuit house were moved to other places where they could receive care. But although Arrupe no longer had to care for visitors' physical needs, he continued to seek to address the spiritual wounds that the faithful retained in the wake of the bombing.

Father Arrupe later spoke of a conversation he had with some young Japanese students. Cynicism gripped the youths as they discussed the force of the bomb that was dropped on Hiroshima and the extent of the loss of life it had caused, and might yet cause. Then an idea came to Arrupe that made a great impression upon the students. He said:

> And after all, my dear friends, in spite of this powerful weapon and any other that may still come, you must know that we have a power much greater than the atomic energy:

14. Lamet, *Pedro Arrupe*, 296.

we have the Heart of Christ. . . . While the atomic energy is destined to destroy and atomize everything, in the Heart of Christ we have an invincible weapon whose power will destroy every evil and unite the minds and hearts of the whole of mankind in one central bond, his love and the love of the Father.[15]

The trust that Father Arrupe held in the Sacred Heart carried him through more than twenty-five years of missionary service in Japan. In 1958, the Society of Jesus elevated Japan from a vice province (that is, a missionary territory) to an autonomous one and made Arrupe its provincial superior. He became an internationally-known figure as he traveled to raise funds for the Japanese province and convince Jesuits from other countries to assist in its work. A Jesuit who met Father Arrupe during a 1954 visit that Arrupe made to Mexico, Father Eduardo Briceño, SJ, remembered him as a powerful spiritual figure: "He was a visionary, a prophet, an apostle, a mixture of Paul, [Francis] Xavier, and Ignatius. He was a man deeply convinced of his mission, and he felt viscerally obliged to carry it out without sparing a moment of his own life."[16]

In May 1965, during the Jesuits' Thirty-First General Congregation, Father Arrupe was elected Superior General of the

---

15. Arrupe, *In Him Alone Is Our Hope*, 115.

16. Lamet, *Pedro Arrupe*, 324.

Society. It was a time of intense change in the church as the Second Vatican Council neared its conclusion. Pope Paul VI, aware that some theologians and liturgists were falsely claiming that certain traditional forms of popular piety contravened the spirit of the Council, asked superiors of religious congregations, including the Jesuits, actively to promote devotion to the Sacred Heart. One of Father Arrupe's first legislative acts as Superior General was to draft a decree, which the General Congregation then passed, in which the Society of Jesus robustly affirmed its agreement with the pontiff's desire that it "spread ever more widely a love for the Sacred Heart of Jesus."

However, as he continued in his role as Superior General, Father Arrupe felt that a stronger statement was needed to counter claims that devotion to the Sacred Heart was too individualistic, given the Council's emphasis on communal liturgical prayer. He therefore wrote a letter to the whole Society in 1972 to mark the centenary of the Society's consecration to the Sacred Heart of Jesus: "Facing a New Situation: Difficulties and Solutions."

As its title suggests, Father Arrupe's letter directly addressed and sought to resolve the "difficulties" associated with the Sacred Heart devotion. One reason for such difficulties, Arrupe wrote, was "the eclipse of sound theological understanding" of Christ's humanity.[17] "The Church is born of the Incarnation," Arrupe explained. "Rather, it is a continuing incarnation; it is the mystical body of God made man. Hence there is nothing less

---

17. Arrupe, *In Him Alone Is Our Hope*, 16.

individualistic than a genuine love of Christ: the very concept of reparation proceeds from an authentic communitarian demand, that of the Mystical Body."[18]

Throughout the years of his active leadership of the Society, until he suffered a stroke in August 1981 that impaired his ability to communicate, Father Arrupe would draw upon the theology of the Sacred Heart to encourage his brother Jesuits and, at times, gently correct them. In a February 1981 address that came to be known as his spiritual testament, he emphasized that "love (service) for our brothers, for Christ, for the Father is the single and indivisible object of our charity"—meaning that true and sacrificial love of neighbor could not be separated from love of God in Jesus Christ.[19]

"Love resolves the dichotomies and tensions that can arise in an imperfectly understood Ignatian spirituality,"[20] Arrupe added. He cited the perceived tension between faith and justice. "Faith has to be informed by charity," he explained, "and so too must justice, which thus becomes a higher form of justice: it is charity that calls for justice."[21] Toward the end of his speech, Father Arrupe spoke frankly about how each person could develop such charity: "There is a tremendous power latent in this devotion to

---

18. Arrupe, *In Him Alone Is Our Hope*, 16.

19. Arrupe, *In Him Alone Is Our Hope*, 148.

20. Arrupe, *In Him Alone Is Our Hope*, 148.

21. Arrupe, *In Him Alone Is Our Hope*, 148.

the Heart of Christ. Each of us should discover it for himself—if he has not already done so—and then, entering deeply into it, apply it to his personal life in whatever way the Lord may suggest and grant."[22]

When Father Arrupe died on February 5, 1991 (having resigned his leadership in 1983 due to infirmity), many believed that his own union with Jesus, which he had exhibited both in sickness and in health, demonstrated the "extraordinary grace" of which he spoke—so much so that a cause for his canonization was opened in 2019, naming him a Servant of God.

Visitors to the Church of the Gesù will find Father Arrupe's tomb in the Chapel of the Passion—an appropriate place for one who sought to unite his heart to the beating Heart of the Savior. The Servant of God's remains are interred in a wall facing the spot where, several chapels down, Pompeo Batoni's painting of the Sacred Heart is ensconced to the right of the main altar.

It is a moving experience to contemplate Arrupe's legacy in the stunningly beautiful shrine church where, on June 9, 1972 (the Solemnity of the Sacred Heart), he celebrated a Mass at which he renewed the consecration of the Society of Jesus to the Sacred Heart of Jesus. But wherever we are, we can make his sentiments our own at Mass: "In this touching Eucharistic celebration, . . . we are going to come into close contact with this truly superatomic source of the Passion of Christ, who is going to offer himself on the altar. May an atom leap from this altar to the wide world, in order that everybody may know Christ's power."[23]

---

22. Arrupe, *In Him Alone Is Our Hope*, 149.

23. Arrupe, *In Him Alone Is Our Hope*, 9. The quote is from Arrupe's May 8, 1970, homily at Valladolid cited earlier in this chapter.

My prayer as I conclude these reflections on holy people who loved the Sacred Heart is that wherever you pray as you seek to draw near to Jesus, whether it is the noblest shrine or the humblest corner, you receive the graces of one who is following in the footsteps of the saints.

Acknowledgments

The author is grateful to Gary Jansen, Maura Poston, Cepheus Edmondson, Elizabeth Lefebvre, and everyone at Loyola Press for their professionalism and dedication in helping bring this book to publication.

About the Author

Dawn Eden Goldstein, JCL, SThD, is one of only a few women to hold both a doctorate in theology licensed by the Holy See and a licentiate in canon law. Dr. Goldstein's books have been translated into ten languages. She lives in Washington, DC.

Devotional Prayer Books

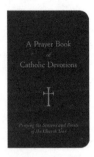

A Prayer Book of
Catholic Devotions
978-0-8294-2030-2

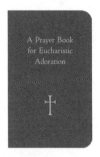

A Prayer Book for
Eucharistic Adoration
978-0-8294-2906-0

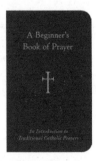

A Beginner's
Book of Prayer
978-0-8294-2792-9

Novenas
978-0-8294-2161-3

To order, call **800.621.1008**, visit **store.loyolapress.com**,
or visit your local bookseller.

Devotional Prayer Books

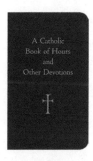

A Catholic Book of Hours and Other Devotions
978-0-8294-2584-0

The Little Office of Jesus and Mary
978-0-8294-4372-1

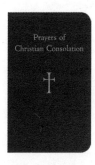

Prayers of Christian Consolation
978-0-8294-2585-7

A Book of Marian Prayers
978-0-8294-3574-0

To order, call **800.621.1008**, visit **store.loyolapress.com**, or visit your local bookseller.